THE ATTRACTIVE TRAP™
Freeing Yourself
From an
Unhealthy Relationship

By
Teresa G. Carey

"Don't be ashamed of your story, it might just inspire someone."

TobyMac #speaklife

The Attractive Trap™ Copyright 2016 Teresa G. Carey
All rights reserved.

TheAttractiveTrap.com

ISBN: 0-9972956-3-4

ISBN-13: 978-0-9972756-3-6

Cover design by Donna Haywood

CONTENTS

REVIEWS AND RECOMMENDATIONS

"This book is wonderfully written and will move so many women from pain into peace."

> —Dawna Daignealt, Ed.S., LPC; Owner, Zest of Life, LLC.; Founder, Ribbon of Worth

"By using relatable examples and offering practical tools, Teresa found an effective way to help women see they deserve to live free from manipulation, abuse, and controlling relationships. I imagine thousands of women reading this book through tears of relief at finally understanding why they feel so trapped and tears of hope for forging a new path. I hope this gets into the hands of ALL the women who so desperately need it!"

> — Sherry Danner, LCMFT, CSAT - Sherry Danner Counseling, LLC

"The stories in the book are powerful and paint a vivid description of each trap. From a therapist's perspective, The Attractive Trap™ is an excellent resource for clients in relationship struggles. From a father/parent perspective, it is an excellent resource for a young adult daughter. Teresa has the gift of bringing awareness and clarity to 'relationship double binds.'"

> — Wayne McKamie, M.Ed., LPC, LCSW; President and Owner, Focus Seminars of Kansas City, LLC

"While affirming God's design for the covenantal permanence of marriage, Teresa navigates with both truth and grace a hopeful path forward for those who find themselves in a badly broken

marriage. Gleaned from a rich storehouse of the author's professional and personal experience, you will discover many golden nuggets of wisdom to guide you on your journey to greater wholeness."

– Dr. Tom Nelson, D.Min.; President, Made To Flourish; Author of "Work Matters: Connecting Sunday Worship to Monday Work," "Five Smooth Stones: Discovering the Path to Wholeness of Soul," and "Ekklesia: Rediscovering God's Design for the Church." Speaker and Facilitator on Faith, Work and Economics; Pastor, Christ Community Church, Leawood, KS

ACKNOWLEDGEMENTS

I continue to stand in awe of the power of timing and opportunity – how just the right people and resources, at just the right time, always seem to collide. For that level of unparalleled brilliance and fortuity, I can only thank my Designer and Creator who has consistently shown me supreme faithfulness, grace and insight.

For all of the women who have lived and dared to tell their journey in these pages to help and inspire others – you are my heroes. I am grateful.

My three children walked this road with me. You have amazed me every day with your strength, courage and persistence in how you do life. I am proud of you and love you in every way.

To my husband, Brett, you have encouraged me and flown with me as my love and eagle since we met and during the conception and birth of this book. You continue to teach me so much about the fascinating dance of how a man loves a woman.

Thank you to my cover designer, and lifetime friend, Donna, as well as my reviewers – Dawna, Sherry, Wayne and Tom. Thank you, Rebecca, for being my advisor. All of you invested a part of yourselves in helping make this a reality. My appreciation overflows.

To you, my readers – we all know women who are caught in the attractive trap™. I am thankful in advance for your assistance in helping women who need to identify and escape this reality that plagues so many relationships. Because of the women in my life who were patient, persistent and loving enough to reveal truth and assistance to me, my life is forever changed. As a tribute to all of you, I vow to always pay forward the opportunity to help women experience freedom, their depth of worth and rawest level of authenticity.

INTRODUCTION

Have you ever lost your voice? I mean the complete loss of your ability to make a sound to communicate verbally? If so, then you absolutely know the hopelessness of the feeling. If not, you can probably imagine it.

Recently, for five long days of complete quiet and helpless silence, I could not utter a single word. Even the slightest attempt at a whisper strained my vocal cords, and the result of any effort was meaningless. For someone who coaches leaders, asks loads of questions, and is expected to sprinkle answers into the mix, this seemed like an abysmal situation. Yet while in this place, I discovered and have since learned there was meaning and purpose to my short time of solitude.

Frustrated and forced only to think and reflect inwardly, my communication was rechanneled into hand gestures and writing. With this limitation, the question quickly became, besides emails and scribbling on the notebook to have a "conversation" with my son, "What should I write?" Upon this reflection, the familiar tug returned. Over the past few years I had felt an ongoing calling to write a book. Now in my forced verbal shut down, at least an attempted start seemed more real and practical than ever.

Just six months before, I had carefully crafted an outline for the book for my niche market and client base. It was still sitting dormant in an electronic file, waiting to be resurrected from the electronic heap. Yet, I couldn't go there and dig it out. Something wouldn't let me. What was keeping me from returning to it?

In my moments of uncertainty and yet wanting to claim my voice, an email came through my inbox. In one eureka moment, my intended course for my subject started to change. The email was from a writing coach, who claimed to have the secret sauce for helping clients be accountable for writing and developing a book. 'What are your obstacles?' 'What's holding you back?' 'What is your topic?' A previous meeting and a degree of familiarity with this cheerleader of the written word prompted me to reach back. "I'm stuck!" I wrote, yet wanted desperately to scream, "I need you! Let's get together!"

So I finally got it. This temporary silence was a gift instead of a curse. This planned timing of sickness and opportunity pushed me down an unexpected path. Or, did it?

Just months prior at a women's conference, I was asked to capture in writing the desires of my heart. I definitively penned that I would write and publish a book, speak about it, and forever change women's lives and hearts about how they see themselves. So, here you have it. The final link of the perfect storm coming together to birth and manifest this delayed start.

Wait. There's one more part to the story. I had to have the experiences to be able to create this work for you, and for me. Although it took losing my voice to force me into taking the first step for sharing this story — the whole truth told — it actually took that occurrence plus the total of 23 years in which I figuratively lost my voice. I allowed my unintended circumstances gradually over time to rob me of speaking and living my truth. I was caught — in a trap. But it was, oh, so attractive. Why would anyone want to be free of such a lovely life?
So before I take you on my journey, and the journey of others who have been in the trap yet are now free, we need to be clear about a few things. Just so there isn't any misunderstanding, please picture me, looking into your eyes.

I do not believe that divorce is God's plan for marriage. I believe that marriage should be sacred, eternal and true. I never wanted or desired to be divorced. I loved my husband and wanted to create a legacy for our children. I wanted to celebrate a 50-year anniversary and then some. In fact, I wanted all of these so badly I was willing to throw away my self-respect and dignity, and forfeit my children's opportunity to see as well how a healthy marriage works — all for the sake of making "IT" work.

What was this "IT" I was holding onto, or caught in – depending on your perspective? How did I get there? What was my moment of realizing I was captive and dying? More importantly, how did I get out? And what did it take to rebuild my life once free from the trap? These are all of the questions I have been called to answer, just for you.

How do I know this? When I met with the writing coach, I was asked a simple question about both topics I was considering. My first answer is barely memorable. It was something like, "I want to write a book for leaders who are…."

My second answer was haunting, because I know it intimately. "My heart beats for women who are caught in the attractive trap – who are in a marriage or relationship that on the outside looks so attractive, but in reality it is severely broken and irreparable."

The woman is trapped. Initially, she doesn't know it, but then she realizes there is a constraint on some part or all of her and over time, the trap is pressing in so much, she doesn't know how she will ever gain her freedom. She has lost most of herself but there is one part left. She just has to find it and use it to break free and move on.

My deepest desire for you, if you are in the attractive trap, is that you will have the insight to know you *are* caught in a place of deceit. With your awakening to the truth, my hope is that you work toward a new place of freedom and press into moving forward and upward with your life. And, most importantly, that you realize the idealism of what you thought was attractive before is truly pale in comparison to the real beauty of rediscovering who you are and the freeing authenticity of what the future can hold for you.

SECTION ONE:

THE CONDITION

"It is hard for a free fish to understand what is happening to a hooked one."

Karl A. Menninger

~CHAPTER ONE~

WHAT IS THE ATTRACTIVE TRAP?

Susan shook her throbbing head in disbelief as she listened to the constant criticism that had just started to creep into their first year of marriage.

"You've lost it. What made you think we could afford that table? You know we don't have the money for that right now. You have to call them first thing in the morning and tell them we're bringing it back, got it?" Mike said, in a ridiculing, parental tone.

What are you talking about? We just decided to buy a table and at that time it was a great idea, Susan questioned inside her head. Knowing the potential backlash, she didn't dare voice her thoughts openly.

Susan's mind went back to their former vivid discussion. "We need to get a table like real people for the kitchen. Let's get on that right away. Why don't you take some time when I'm out of town next week to go shop for one?" *There. You have it. Mike did say this just over a week ago, didn't he?*

Susan and Mike had been talking about buying a kitchen table for their current bare kitchen. It had been recently claimed as a top priority on the list of "must haves" for the house. Since moving in their house just five months ago, Susan and Mike both agreed they were tired of sitting on the sofa to eat or using the old dining room table Susan had brought into the marriage.

While Mike was on another business trip, she had found the 100-year-old treasure at a local antique show for less than they had discussed spending. Knowing they had made the decision to buy, coupled with landing the perfect find at the right price, Susan felt she made a decision she could be proud of.

Now, unexpectedly, Mike's disapproval layered on over their place of agreement, caused Susan's head to throb like the rhythm of a freight train rolling down the track. Mike had to leave town again which made her upset deepen in the midst of unresolved conflict. She was left to battle within her own mind.

Susan felt a camouflage of confusion. However, she knew as she searched within her rationalizing thoughts that she shouldn't be confused any more than she should have been reprimanded. She had simply acted on their decision to buy a household necessity. Susan was at war in her head. Why was Mike doing this?

> *And at some undefined tipping point, those attractive objects begin to define us until we become a part of them.*

Mike hadn't been this upset so far in their one year of marriage. She had seen signs of control and a critical nature in Mike, yet this surpassed the other signs to date. He had been upset when dinner wasn't quite up to his standards or laundry wasn't folded as expected. Sometimes he didn't show up for dinner when promised and was never apologetic or concerned about it. Yet this was the deepest cut at her judgment and performance so far. Shame poured over Susan like rain falling from a cloudburst.

Susan knew in her heart and her head this wasn't just a normal marital disagreement over the purchase of a table. The diminishing of her decision-making ability, her intellect as well as her intent had once again unfolded. It just had the addition of a different character in the play – Susan, Mike, and now a kitchen table.

Susan knew she had caused a ripple of disappointment through the one person she craved to please. Her heart was broken. She cried herself to sleep hoping she would never cause Mike to question her discernment or desire to do the right thing again. A feeling of powerlessness overcame her. She knew she was supposed to please the man she married. She wanted to be perfect for him in every way, just like she knew he expected. The right food cooked in the right way. The most attractive clothes worn the most pleasing way. The cleanest house in the most impeccable order. Check. Check. Check.

Susan knew what she had to do. She would call the shop owner the next day and explain they couldn't afford the table. She would say she misunderstood the budget she and Mike had planned. She would ask for the antique dealer's forgiveness as a newlywed who didn't yet understand what had been agreed upon. It could simply be chalked up to poor communication between two people who were just getting to know how to do life together. "That's it!" Susan tried to reconcile. Problem solved. Yet Susan knew she could never make such a grave mistake again in letting down Mike.

When we continuously overcompensate even in the early stages of a relationship just to keep peace, we are headed to a place of entanglement.

> *When we continuously overcompensate even in the early stages of a relationship just to keep peace, we are headed to a place of entanglement.*

It's intriguing how something can look so good on the outside, yet underneath the surface, it's completely different. Think about a beautiful swan on a lake. It is so calm, graceful, and lovely gliding along the surface of the calm water. Yet no one sees what's happening underneath. The feet are paddling busily to stay afloat. Others only see what's above the surface, not below. The swan unconsciously makes the kicking effort seem natural without even realizing the extreme effort in motion to stay afloat.

Relationships and families are the same. On the outside, it can all look picture perfect. Pull together a big house, 2.5 kids, new cars, the country club membership, prime positioning on the church pew, and successful jobs – as just a few of the starting ingredients for the savory recipe. Blended together, all of these things can be made to look so attractive they are hard to give up. They can start to trump the insanity of what a healthy life and relationship should be like. And at some undefined tipping point, those attractive objects begin to define us until we are part of them.

BREAKTHROUGH MOMENTS

- In what ways have you started to lose or have you already lost your voice in your current relationship?

- What about the relationship causes you to feel powerless?

- How has your judgment or decision-making been unnecessarily questioned?

- How has this eroded your confidence?

- What are the attractive things in your life you don't want to give up?

BREAK AWAY THOUGHTS

- You were fearfully and wonderfully made with a worthy voice and mind. Being in a relationship doesn't mean you have to give that power away. A healthy partner and mate wants you to express your voice and yourself and never tries to diminish or squelch it.

- When others question your judgment after you have invested much time and energy in evaluating and acting on your best efforts, their questioning behavior is about their issues, more than yours.

- No earthly object, image or perception is worth losing yourself over. Things are always replaceable. Recapturing your self-respect is harder work than regaining possessions.

~CHAPTER TWO~

THINGS AREN'T ALWAYS AS THEY APPEAR

Connie wandered in a daze out of the doctor's office, once again puzzled. Another STD? How could this happen? She knew she had been faithful to her husband in every way.

The first STD had been bad enough with both the stigma and embarrassment of venereal warts. Both she and Brad listened as the doctor said, "Sometimes this happens. It's no big deal." As she reflected, it seemed strangely odd that Brad didn't seem more surprised, disappointed or vocal about the discovery.

But to Connie, it was a surprise, a disappointment, and absolutely starting to feel like a big deal. And now a diagnosis of Chlamydia? Although fear was rampant throughout her heart and mind, denial was still her protector. This was unimaginable. She served as the care pastor of a large church. Brad, a respected and upright man in the church, was a deacon. Their twins, Steven and Sean, were leaders in the youth group and participated in all the church activities. The pieces of this puzzle weren't fitting together – at least on the surface.

Connie couldn't possibly imagine any improper behavior on her husband's part. She was sure he was the faithful man he professed to be.

Or was he?

> *When you have more questions than answers, check your reality. Maybe you're hiding behind a curtain of denial.*

Yet the compelling evidence lay before her. Lots of it. Papers about the Chlamydia treatment she needed fanned out across the passenger seat of her car. In two weeks, she would check into the hospital for an outpatient procedure, cryotherapy – the freezing of the cervix to kill any infected cells. Then she would require a round of antibiotics and abstinence from any sexual activity for several cycles until she thoroughly healed.

Fear engulfed her. How could she possibly explain this to the church elders and the other deacons? One of the deacons' wives, April, worked as a nurse at the hospital. Connie was certain she would find out about the procedure. Would the rules of confidentiality keep April from teasing her husband with the unexpected question of intrigue, "Guess who has a sexually-transmitted disease?"

After that, what would happen? Connie's throat tightened. Would the elders and the other pastors believe her if she told them she had faithfully kept her marriage vows? And if *she* had been faithful, then that meant Brad …. This was almost more than Connie could process. How could this be happening?

Tiny chards of reality from the broken glass house began to trickle into Connie's subconscious. Wait. What about the magazine she found a month ago in Brad's car? All of those lewd and raunchy images made her stomach churn. As she was trying to figure out how they could have landed within her world, she confronted Brad. He simply explained in his convincing manner, "Uh-oh. Our boys must be messing around with things they shouldn't be. I'll have a talk with them. Don't worry."

But Connie *was* worried. Actually, worry was an understatement. She started to question and finally listened to the spirit inside her, "Connie, do you really believe it was the boys?"

Hold on. Connie knew this dance of self-awareness. After all, she counseled other women! She mentally ticked off the advice she gave other wives who came to her for counseling when they suspected their husbands were unfaithful: 1) be courageous 2) set up your own checking account – just in case he decides to leave 3) set personal boundaries and 4) check into resources at your church.

Connie immediately started to rationalize why she may not be able to take some of her own advice. What kind of resources could she depend on? She couldn't even go for counseling without the entire town and the church finding out about it. And she knew exactly what would happen if by some strange happenstance all of this was true.

The care pastor's job description allowed no room for divorce or even separation. Marital "bliss" was a requirement of the job.

If this nightmare turned out to be true, she would lose her job, the ministry she loved, and her beloved twin boys would be devastated. She would end up not only a single mom, but an unemployed single mom with two boys to parent on her own.

She couldn't possibly condemn her boys to that kind of life. But what else could she do? Continue to live with Brad and look the other way? Forgive him and endure the treatment for yet another STD?

Somehow, Connie couldn't believe God would want her to do that.

Types of Traps – Not All Are Created Equal

Clearly, Connie's case presents yet another form of the trap. Being in denial, in spite of all the glaring and obvious evidence, yet still not yielding to reality, shines a light on this trap. Connie's reliance on her marriage for her job, the "reputation" of their marriage to others in the church and community, her own need to feel it was a great marriage and Brad was a respectable man, all played into the façade of the trap.

Traps are just that – a seemingly attractive way to secure something by being mistaken for something else. Otherwise, why would a fully-aware and knowing person allow themselves to get caught?

Traps work well because of the way they are designed. Just as there are different traps for different animals, so there are parallel traps for people and reasons they work so well.

What are these traps?

The Snare Trap

Snare Traps are generally made of light wire cable looped through a locking device or of a small nylon cord tied so that it will tighten as the animal pulls against it. The more a snared animal struggles, the tighter the noose becomes; the tighter the noose, the greater the animal's struggle and suffering. In an "attractive" relationship, the more the woman who is trapped tries to speak her voice, confront the issues and exert her own control as a way to break free, the control of the trap and trapper are tightened and amplified.

It was a calm and uneventful night. Sharon knew that feeling… yet there was an uneasiness to the night of alleged normalcy. The calm always came before the storm that was brewing in the atmosphere. What would she say or do that would create the perfect storm for the imperfect outcome of the night? What would the tipping point or snare be tonight for saying the wrong thing at just the right time? Then, it happened − when the moment should have been most peaceful − at bedtime.

While nestled on the bed for nighttime stories, Matt stopped by the room for the routine hug and kiss goodnight from their five-year-old daughter. Being absent for work more than 70 percent of the time didn't allow for this luxury often, so it was the right thing to do.

When Paige excitedly told her dad about her soccer kick that day that landed a goal, he went into a halo of praise. "You are the athlete in the family… you are the best athlete out of all our children." Matt beamed.

Sharon gulped. Could their sons in the other room hear? Would the older son who struggled with confidence in life and athleticism due to social issues be privy to this proclamation?

Quietly and without calculated thought Sharon whispered, "Please don't compare our kids. That's like your mother comparing you and your sister. Let's not do that…."

But before she could complete the sentence, there it was — swiftly and shockingly. Like the ball Paige kicked confidently on the soccer field that morning, yet with a much stronger force, Matt's size-13 foot landed onto the bone of Sharon's left hip.

Stunned, Paige and Sharon weren't sure whether they should pretend it didn't happen or start the tornado siren to signal there had just been a major touchdown with damage in sight. Trained as peacekeepers, they both held back the tears, remained stoic and continued to finish the tale of Angelina Ballerina.

The next day, Matt demanded he would never be talked to that way again, and that his mother could never be insulted like that — as though something dishonoring had been said versus a rule of engagement in not comparing their children. This was more of his same behavior — twisting the truth to try in some strange way to justify his actions.

The Guarded Trap

Guarded Traps have a spring-loaded guard attachment to prevent whatever is trapped from escaping or injuring itself while trying to escape. These traps often are used when seeking certain animals such as muskrats in shallow water where a killing device may not work.

That's good news for the trapper! A killing device isn't wanted in an attractive trap scenario because there wouldn't be anything left to control. The main idea is to just trap the person and keep her guarded until the trapper "releases" her. However, in an unhealthy relationship, the trap keeps getting set and the escape doesn't injure the woman physically. Like the muskrat, when you keep swimming in the same pond where the guarded trap exists, you will invariably get caught again. The trap always stays in place.

Each time Jessica tried to break free from her controlling relationship with Ted, his initial reaction was to cry and tell her he didn't understand why she wouldn't want to be with him. True to form, Jessica would give in and succumb to Ted's plea. Then, as usual, Ted used his wealth as a snare trap. He would buy her a piece of jewelry or plan an exotic vacation, reminding her none of this was as bad as she thought. Ted used not only gifts but sex as a snare, wanting to "make love" at least a few times daily — just another trap of control to remind Jessica he loved and adored only her. The more Jessica tried to get away, the more Ted upped the ante to make sure she stayed.

The Cage Trap

Like a Guarded Trap, the **Cage Trap** is placed along a runway or common path. Bait exists in a cage trap, depending on the survival mode of the animal. The bait may be food the animal needs or even bait that temporarily numbs, stuns or disables the animal.

Nikki was a strong woman who emerged from a lineage of enviable females. They were smart, confident and high-achieving. This was exactly the type of wife Robert needed and wanted. By baiting and controlling Nikki, he would achieve his dream of taming a self-assured woman.

In this second attempt at marriage, Nikki felt the pressure of getting it right this time. She still carried shame from the crumbling of her first marriage. She was determined to get a man who she didn't overpower or intimidate.

Knowing how important her faith and winning at this second marriage was to her, Robert used both of these predictably to make Nikki believe she had to be a "submissive wife" to be a good wife. He twisted and contextualized this often confusing principle in a way to make her think she didn't have the power she had previously been taught and felt.

Nikki's work travel was consistent for a couple of days each week, and each time she would come home, it was like going down the same path over and over again. Robert would go through the ritual with her to make sure she knew he was in charge by giving his usual speech demanding that she give him all her time and attention. He would play the victim, and he always enjoyed reminding Nikki how she had inconvenienced him by being gone once again.

Robert knew how to diminish Nikki by using guilt and condemnation to compromise her self- awareness of her worth as a wife and mother. By playing on these two most vulnerable areas consistently, he was accomplishing his goal of breaking her down and keeping her in his cage.

The Ant Trap

With **Ant Traps**, special baits attract the insects to eat foods containing insecticides that kill them. To make the traps work properly, it is important to keep the areas where all the food is stored clean. When there is no other food around, the insects concentrate only on the bait, not on other foods they like better. What is the trick of using such traps? It is in making sure that the ants find the bait, eat it and take some of it back to the queen and others in the nest.

The worker ants, of course, are completely unaware of the poison they are spreading to the rest of the colony. But over time, the harm is done. The other ants have ingested the poison and are dead.

Dana kept going back to the trap, because what she was being fed there seemed to be palatable – for a while. Until, unwittingly, the poison from the trap started to be internalized by the others in the home.

Just a year later, Dana's son starting doing drugs to numb the pain, and the bait was spread throughout the home. Finally through a series of harmful family events, Dana realized this was a trap of perpetuity. Until she left the trap, she would continue to carry the poison of Tom's abusive and ambiguous behavior as well as her own resentment and anger to the others in the home.

The ones who deserved to live and live fully couldn't thrive if they kept being fed the poisonous bait from the trap.

BREAKTHROUGH MOMENTS

Below are the Definitive Ten Signs you are caught in a trap:

- You have more questions than answers about the relationship.

- You are consistently trying to convince yourself that the marriage or relationship is right for you.

- You are staying in the marriage only because you feel it is best for someone else.

- You've become certain you will lose your reputation if you leave the relationship.

- You have to tell lies to yourself and/or to others about the relationship.

- You are staying in the relationship for money or some other "charm" factor.

- You question your self-worth. You feel diminished instead of multiplied when you are with the person.

- You see continued patterns that are diametrically opposed – either charm or harm.

- You are staying for religious reasons or because you feel you will be ostracized spiritually or by an organized group from your church or temple.

- You are told by the other person you don't have options, no one will want you because you're not good enough or you have kids, or any other false, manipulative reason.

BREAK AWAY THOUGHTS

- Listen to and honor your instinct, your inner guide and the Spirit.

- Surround yourself with wise counsel with whom you can start to vet and validate your thoughts.

- Recognize that most trappers have one trap they prefer. Once used, it will be utilized over and over. To be a learner, you only need one lesson. Do not become a student. Get the one lesson, the only one needed, and get out of the trap.

~CHAPTER THREE~

HOW DO WE END UP TRAPPED?

Love at Any Price

Carol always wanted to feel loved, secure and protected by a man. Growing up in a house of five boys with lots of family time, religious upbringing as well as love and laughter, one would assume security would reign. However, instead of feeling safe, Carol was often the object of ridicule and teasing from her brothers.

Carol's mom, although very present, chalked it up as "brotherly love." And with eight kids to raise, she didn't have the luxury of managing every behavior. She was tired from all the activity, so only the issues in the family that she deemed critical and family-impacting were addressed.

Carol's father? He was a ball of energy, a serial entrepreneur and a workaholic. Carol adored him. Although Carol knew he loved her, the reality was he simply didn't and often couldn't carve out the time Carol craved. His numerous business ventures and family responsibilities trumped Carol's innate longing for affection.

Unfortunately, this backdrop set the stage for how Carol would respond in her relationships with men. If all of these life pieces fit together at an opportune time, Carol's insecurities could be wittingly observed by the wrong man – one in pursuit of her vulnerability in male relationships – one who would lay the bait for her to fall prey to control, manipulation and ultimately – abuse.

Carol didn't have a boyfriend in high school. She was too involved in sports, church and activities. After graduation, Carol's boyish and athletic body burgeoned into a stunning and eye-catching work of art. With a voluptuous figure, striking face and playful personality, it didn't take long for the catch of the town to notice her.

Rob was branded by his unparalleled charm and looks. When he started pursuing Carol, she was surprised and caught off guard. Carol's naiveté, one of her enduring qualities, masked many things, such as her awareness of unknowingly attracting attention. One of Carol's coworkers tipped her off, and soon Rob was stopping by the store to get her attention.

Carol was dumbfounded and began to wonder, why does the most coveted guy in town want to date me?

Not only did he persistently attempt to win her favor with flowers, gifts and nonstop affection, Rob moved aggressively to make sure she married him. Within nine months, Rob had proposed. Within a year and a half, Carol had finally landed the certainty of a lifelong commitment from a man – exactly what she had longed for.

Shortly after, the courting stopped and the spiral toward what seemed like insanity ensued. "You stupid bitch!" the voice screamed from another room.

The words made Carol's chest tighten and her heart quicken. Did she hear correctly? The shock caused her to think she had misunderstood the words. Had the TV channel been switched to HBO, and she was merely overhearing a dramatic scene from an abusive movie? But wait – that was Rob's voice. She spun around to see him angrily walking into the room.

Within the next few seconds, Carol realized she must have done something so wrong, she deserved this abusive dig. Rob had never said anything ugly to her before. Maybe he was just having a bad day.

Then Rob spat more venom, revealing the provocation for his outburst – a partially melted quart of ice cream.

Carol started to concede that she had made a careless and dumb mistake. Her mind rewound to age 13 when her brother called her stupid for burning the pancakes while their parents were gone. That had to be the problem – simply a combination of Rob's stressful day and her stupidity. She was sure he would never say anything so ugly again. After all, they were just words.

She had learned how to protect herself from abusive words many years before.

Carol was wrong. Name-calling soon became commonplace and Rob's typical way of communication. Rob seemed increasingly frustrated after a long day at work. In her mind, Carol negotiated all of Rob's behaviors. She consistently reconciled the balance sheet by remembering all the good times they shared and all the great ways he helped around the house. After plodding through the same equation, she kept returning to the fact that Rob had never laid a hand on her. Wasn't that *real* abuse?

> *Abuse can happen gradually over time as we mistake a person's use of control for an unusual level of concern. These are not the same.*

Within two years, they had two kids. Carol was convinced Rob must love her because he provided so well for the family. The nasty comments continued, and within months, Rob was waiting for Carol when she got home from work. He checked her mileage to make sure she hadn't driven outside the boundaries of her round trip to work. When Rob got home, if Carol was there, he would touch the hood of her car, checking its warmth to make sure she hadn't left while he was away. This felt like unnecessary control, yet Carol knew Rob loved her or he wouldn't care so much.

Carol continually circled back to the affirmation that Rob was the greatest catch in the area, so she had to hang on to him. She would be crazy to let him go. She was compelled to always prove to Rob, to others and especially to herself – that she was worthy of this man's love.

Conditioned to be Trapped

Family Modeling

How did Carol end up so blind to Rob's behavior? Telling this story today, Carol admits she can hardly believe she was so self-deceived and trapped. While Rob deceived Carol, she also deceived herself. And it didn't start with the day she met Rob or the day she walked down the aisle. She was set up much earlier in life for believing Rob's behavior toward her was acceptable.

The adage, children learn what they live, could never be more true as in this example. To a large degree, Carol's mother was controlled. She bore and raised eight children, which made certain there were some boundaries about what she could and could not do.

"We have to continually remind ourselves that in an abusive household, the daughter grows up seeing abuse as 'normal' (Psychology Today, Dale Archer, M.D. August 5, 2013).

With today's exposure to the rampant and evolving diversity of behaviors prevalent on mainstream and social media, we have become desensitized to what the acceptable treatment of others should look like.

One in four women in the US are the victims of physical violence, according to The National Domestic Violence Hotline (2014). The findings continue by reporting that nearly half of all women and men in the United States have experienced psychological aggression by an intimate partner in their lifetime. The problem is revealed in how we define abuse.

The Department of Justice is crystal clear on its definition. In a statement issued in July, 2014 they stated, "We define **domestic violence** as a pattern of abusive behavior in any relationship that is used by one partner to gain or maintain power and control over another intimate partner. **Domestic violence** can be physical, sexual, emotional, economic, or psychological actions or threats of actions that influence another person."

The National Domestic Abuse Hotline sums it up this way, "Many abusive partners may seem absolutely perfect in the early stages of a relationship. Possessive and controlling behaviors don't always appear overnight, but rather emerge and intensify as the relationship grows."

Domestic violence doesn't look the same in every relationship because every relationship is different. But one thing most abusive relationships have in common is that the abusive partner does many different kinds of things to have more power and control over his partner.

The behaviors identified by multiple sources as signs of abuse include:

✓ Twists the facts
✓ Misleads / lies
✓ Avoids taking responsibility
✓ Withholds information
✓ Craves and demands control
✓ Makes up his own rules
✓ Demands forgiveness
✓ Masquerades as someone of noble character
✓ Emotionally detached
✓ Guilty gift-giving
✓ Denies reality
✓ No evidence of growth or change
✓ Rejects accountability
✓ Uses religion /scripture to put down women
✓ Forceful sexual advances / rape
✓ Abuses pets
✓ Demands submissiveness
✓ Expert at creating confusion

"Abuse is simply behavior that seeks to control the other person in any way. Sandra Horley CBE, Chief Executive of the National Domestic Violence Charity Refuge, reminds us, "The aim of the behavior is to take control. It's confusing because the abuser can be so charming." Research among young women shows that while 95% of women recognize physical abuse as domestic violence, just over a quarter of them in most studies know about the more subtle signs of a controlling relationship. We talk about *domestic violence* and tend to understand those lines, yet the boundaries around *domestic abuse* seem more blurred. Or are they?

Let's revisit Susan from chapter one. In reality, the predisposition for her remorse about buying the table started much sooner than their first married year. Susan vividly recalled when she was a young girl; she would watch her father ridicule her mother for making purchases. Susan's mother bought needed clothes and shoes for herself and the kids, then secretly ushered them into the house when her husband was away or sleeping.

> *Part of the challenge is that we have become desensitized to what the acceptable treatment of others should actually look like.*

She learned that even the smallest purchases and decisions may not be up for proper approval.

The dance observed in relationships is imprinted early on. The problem presents itself as no distinction between what constitutes healthy and unhealthy relationships. As mothers and fathers, we teach our daughters what boundaries and behaviors we will or will not tolerate.

As described in their bestselling work, "Boundaries: When to Say Yes, How to Say No," Drs. Henry Cloud and John Townsend make it clear. The notion of boundaries in all our lives and in every area is pervasive. Physical boundaries define how we will be touched and who is allowed to touch us. Emotional boundaries define our emotional intelligence and protect us from the controlling of emotions by others. Mental boundaries help us feel the liberation of having our own thoughts, opinions and voice.

How many of us while growing up have heard an uncle, aunt or grandparent remark, "Wow, you're gaining weight!" Or they "innocently" tease us about our characteristics or habits. One person repeatedly heard her father say to their family friends, "She doesn't like boys…" or "She's not as smart as her brothers…" Even these cues early in life trick us into believing those types of diminishing comments are just a normal part of family reunion or kitchen table conversation and should be tolerated.

Unless we as parents teach our children, and in this case our daughters, to have a voice for themselves in every situation, we can set the stage for their believing that personal comments woven of the smallest of attacking threads are normal. We need to get our daughters in touch with their feelings, helping them recognize hurt for what it is – a legitimate, real and validated feeling. It is appropriate and even necessary to respond with, "Please don't say that to me," or "That makes me feel uncomfortable."

> *Family or societal induced- shame tied to leaving or divorce can be as powerful as personal shame causing us to stay in a relationship.*

Societal Expectations

In addition to the behaviors modeled by family members, society often doesn't do girls and women any favors.

"Domestic abuse," says Horley, "is a reflection, on an individual scale, of how women are treated on a larger scale in society. It's subtle, cumulative and often, but not always, first shows itself when a woman makes a commitment to a man." The abuse, she goes on to explain, is gradual and the man manipulates the woman into thinking it is her fault, that she is to blame.

It's often that subtle place where unhealthy "love" spills over into possessiveness, jealousy and even envy of the other person.

A study conducted by sociologist Heidi Fischer Bjelland, a PhD student at The Norwegian Police University College found that contrary to what many may surmise, women who have a higher income or education than their partners are far more likely to suffer psychological abuse and domestic violence. Research observing thousands of couples found the stereotype of powerful men abusing their socially weaker partner did not stand up.

"Whenever power is unevenly allocated in a relationship the chance of physical and psychological abuse increases," said Bjelland. "And the abused partner is the one with the highest status. Violence or control is used as a compensation for the partner's weak position, in the relationship, and may thus be regarded as an attempt to balance what is perceived as an uneven division of power." Bjelland examined survey replies from 1640 men and 1791 women who lived with their partners.

Ironic, isn't it? Many of the women who may not "need" men are the ones caught in the trap. They are smart, powerful, and have great potential, yet feel they need to be loved. Perhaps the overachievement in life and work over-compensates for the lack of self-worth. The overpowering spouse sees something of worth within them that they don't even see themselves. That's why it's important to continue to put them in their place and keep them down.

Of course, not every woman who is in the trap is high-achieving, blessed with status or up-to-date job skills. Yet the commonality is most likely mired in a deficit of self-worth – the one thing all women in the trap share.

In a website featuring an organization called "EMPOW**HER**MENT," published to promote the empowerment of women, the writers remind us, "All we have to do is look around at the messaging that happens outside the home." In a recent article they wrote that "society still tells us that women should want to be in relationships because healthy relationships are essential for happiness and women will regret being alone. Not all of this is a conscious message but in many cases, it is implied."

So society tells us a relationship at any price in any trap is better than no relationship at all.

Religious Rules and Misunderstandings

"The church kept me trapped..." is one of the most common sentiments expressed by those who have allowed religion to keep them in the confines of an unhealthy relationship. "I thought God hated divorce and I was pleasing him by staying in the marriage – for better or for worse."

With a legalistic and strict religious upbringing, Darcy didn't ever believe divorce was an option. Growing up, she had heard disdain both in the church services and in the home regarding the "sin" of divorce. In spite of the name-calling, constant criticism, Stu acting as if he was going to hit her and eventually shoving and kicking her, she never felt the church or God would approve of her escape.

The words of the Ten Commandments flooded her mind, "Thou shalt not bear false witness/lie...." Wait, wasn't this marriage a lie? Wasn't she hiding something in public that wasn't true in private?

"Thou shalt not commit adultery." Hold on; is the act of adultery limited to an act with another person? What if my husband is so in love with himself, drugs and alcohol more than his wife, that a female adulteress would almost be welcomed?

With the usual "adultery" violation, at least the church would "legitimately" excuse her choice to leave the marriage. Darcy was caught – and this trap was the omniscient, omnipresent, omnivorous church in her mind.

The thought of being ostracized caused fear to consume and paralyze her. Remember Connie in chapter two? As a minister in the church, even with an "excused reason" she still lost her job because the letter "D" for divorce was permanently etched on her sweater and eventually her tombstone. No better than Hester she would conclude, reflecting on Nathaniel Hawthorne's 1850 work, "The Scarlet Letter" bridled with a theme of legalism, sin and guilt.

The conundrum for Darcy continued. How could they believe she was better off unhappy and destined to a life of continued betrayal instead of breaking free to a life of freedom and renewed hope?

It was only after confessing her husband's emotional, mental and escalating physical abuse to her pastor that Darcy was told to separate and pray for her Stu to repent. What if Stu didn't repent or truly change? Would she still be free to file for divorce? Somehow the internal messaging from years of hearing "divorce is wrong" wouldn't leave the recesses of her mind, in spite of the green light given from her counselors.

Finally, a message from a counselor provided a breakthrough. "Marriages are not worth saving, people are. When both people in the marriage can be saved, then the marriage is worth rescuing."

Another Christian friend and prayer partner finally joined in with, "God came to save people and to set the captive free, not to save marriage."

Kassie's husband was obsessive compulsive and wanted to control everything, except what mattered most. Kassie took on those things. She over-functioned in the marriage with four kids to make sure everyone was taken care of. The verbal and mental abuse escalated throughout their 20-year marriage.

Active as a volunteer in the youth ministry, Kassie was bound to abide by the church's rule of no divorce for paid or volunteer leaders in the church. When she mustered up the courage to speak her truth and started moving in the direction to set herself free from a miserable and abusive marriage, she summed up her hold-back for all those years. "It's funny how the people who are supposed to love me as part of my faith community would rather see me miserable on the church pew in the fourth row every Sunday than see me thriving and happy, though divorced."

Darcy and Kassie have more company. In chapter two, Connie described it similarly by describing how her religious affiliation impacted her false need to stay in her deceived relationship:

"One of the direct messages I got from the 'church' was that if I married a Christian, everything would work out. Only 'nonChristians' or misguided and desperate women who were Christians but married nonbelievers got divorced. The indirect message – also from the church – was that only married people got to belong in groups and be accepted. There were no programs for singles, and I'm from the era where a single woman older than 21 was an 'old maid.' So you didn't really 'belong' if you were single. You had to find Prince Charming in order to be truly accepted.

"Fortunately, some churches now have viable singles groups, but I still have not heard a sermon that encourages people to remain single or to use their single status – whether unmarried or divorced – to further the Kingdom. I find that incredibly sad, but most churches focus their programs on the traditional family."

She goes on to share, "I'm not sure my parents really fostered these messages, but then we never talked about it either. And since they were part of the church, I assumed they accepted without question what the church believed."

International author and writer Laura Petheridge, in her recent article on Crosswalk.com (April 17, 2015), entitled, *Why God Really Hates Divorce,* summed it up this way. According to her observation and personal experience, the big three that cause divorce are – addiction, adultery and abuse. Petheridge writes, "Most of the church-related marriage classes focus on Venus and Mars, communication, respect, and intimacy. Those are great subjects for the couples who merely need a 'tune up.' However, when issues such as pornography, abuse, manipulation, drugs or alcohol, or an extramarital affair are involved – those classes don't work. Ironically, they can exacerbate the problem because the offender often uses the class to his/her advantage."

Saving Our Daughters – Building Their Self Worth

Do we talk to our daughters about this? What messages are we sending to help them be discerning through the maze of courtship and ultimately in selecting the person they will share life with? Do we arm them to recognize and address the signs in any relationship that are abusive?

In the book, "Raising a Princess: Eight Essential Virtues to Teach Your Daughter," Big Oak Ranch founder John Croyle draws on 40 years of parenting 2,000 children.

According to an article about Croyle's book featured on AL.com, he states, "Obviously, raising a little girl, you're dealing with the emotional factor," Croyle said. "Girls are a lot more emotional than boys."

Certain traits need to be taught to both boys and girls, and some distinct to each, he said. "Some things are absolutes – manners, class, integrity," Croyle said. "Girls need a special kind of nurturing.

"So many girls don't know what a real young woman looks like," Croyle said. "The key is letting a girl know she's praiseworthy. She doesn't have to perform or look a certain way. She's been given traits and gifts that are praiseworthy. If you tell a girl she's ugly, stupid, not worth anything, she'll believe it. If you tell her, 'You have value, you have self-esteem,' she'll believe it. Every little girl is worthy of praise."

In a perfect world, we are developing self-esteem. What are we teaching our daughters about relationships?

Adele, who will share her story in Chapter Four, is teaching her five girls, aged 5 to 17, to first and foremost protect their hearts. She tells them the reason she had to leave their dad is because she knew her heart was worth protecting. Adele says, "If there is a behavior someone uses that you know feels wrong to you in your heart, then it's wrong." Anything that makes you feel diminished is out of line. What simple yet vital advice for our girls to remember and carry with them for a lifetime!

Today's society wants girls to "just suck it up" convincing them they are often too sensitive. They're told they need to step up, lean in, or do whatever it takes to be on equal footing. Instead of WWJD (What Would Jesus Do?), the expectation is warped to filter their reaction through the lens of WWMD (What Would a Man Do?)

What do we teach our daughters, especially in light of Bjelland's research about how an uneven balance of power can cause the abuser to abuse and even escalate his behavior? Absolutely the answer is NOT to earn less or have less power. The lesson is to choose wisely. To choose a secure man who is not intimidated by having a lower status or compensation, or allows his insecurities about his physical state or any other part of his being to influence how he treats others.

We can teach our daughters attributes about finding men who are secure and emotionally well enough to be with a woman – regardless of her economic status or power level. According to Dr. Shannon Kolakowski, Psychologist and Author, the following provides hints to identifying those who are emotionally well. And she adds, "Most of us will continue to cultivate these qualities throughout our lives, as opposed to ever reaching a point where we stop and say, 'Okay, I'm done now – I've reached emotional wellness.' "

1- **He will treat others well.** Having sensitivity to the needs of others, empathy and relatability with everyone from the waitress to the co-worker says a lot about a person's emotional bandwidth.

2- **He likes and knows himself.** Being the same person inside in private as well as in public rings of authenticity as does living the life he wants versus what someone else wants.

3- **He's flexible.** Adaptability and the response to unexpected life situations is a sign of how a person will surface emotionally to all kinds of circumstances life may present.

4- **He's grateful for loved ones, regardless of differences.** The emphasis is on being appreciative. As emotionally healthy beings, communicating and showing gratitude is anchored to relationship well-being.

5- **He's in touch with his emotions. Embracing both positive and negative emotions are seen as a natural part of life.**

6- **He has a greater purpose and meaning to life.** Leading a purposeful life is about having a passion, a mission or a larger meaning to life.

7- **He values experiences (and people) in his life more than possessions.** While having goals and a drive for attainment is fine, those who place a higher value on wealth, popularity, or attractiveness tend to be less well-off emotionally than people who value self-fulfillment and being there for others.

If another person or relationship causes us to compromise ourselves and our worth to the extent that we minimize our true feelings, numb ourselves out and discount ourselves for the sake of the other person or relationship, then we are pleasing others instead of the girl in the glass.

So with such brazen examples, why don't women leave? It's simple. Every behavior we execute is based on fear or desire. Clearly, we are afraid. The fear is paralyzing. The fear creates confusion. Fear is the birthplace of anger and deep hurt. To protect ourselves, we numb the hurt so it doesn't seem so bad after all.

Between the modeling from family and parents, and the messaging from society and religion or church, we get stuck. The fear is so strong and overwhelming, it overrides our sensibility regarding logic or what is real.

And so we stay. Or not....

BREAKTHROUGH MOMENTS

- What messages or modeling did you receive as a child that influenced your male relationships?

- What was the picture you formed in your mind about how your future relationships would look or what you would aspire to? How is this idealism keeping you trapped?

- How has your religious affiliation influenced your thoughts about what is morally right? How has this kept you trapped?

- In retrospect, how has this caused you to make the choices you have made in your relationships (i.e., "I gave myself to him sexually so now I have to stay with him and/or marry him even though I see an abusive pattern")?

- If you could take just one step today to face your fear and move toward freedom, what would it be?

45

BREAK AWAY THOUGHTS

- All of us were conditioned toward many life and relationship choices. Ultimately, we decide how we handle the choices given to us.

- You don't have to make the break away all at once (unless you or your children are in danger). Create your plan and start to implement it. Now. Chapter Four will give you some tools.

- By doing one thing each day to move toward freedom, you are making progress. Pick your one thing each day to give yourself hope in moving closer to your overall goal.

RESOURCES

"Psychology Today," Dale Archer, M.D., August 5, 2013

The National Domestic Violence Hotline, 2014

www.leslievernick.com

"Boundaries: When to Say Yes, How to Say No," by Dr. Henry Cloud and Dr. John Townsend, 2008

EMPOWHERMENT.com

"Why God Really Hates Divorce," by Laura Petheridge, Crosswalk.com, April 17, 2015

"Raising a Princess: Eight Essential Virtues to Teach Your Daughter," John Croyle, 2014

SECTION TWO:
THE TRANSITION

"A truth bomb is a truth that shakes a person into reality."

Danielle LaPorte

~CHAPTER FOUR~

RELEASING YOURSELF FROM THE TRAP

The Awakening

As the youngest of three, a perpetual parent pleaser, and designated peacekeeper, Adele was primed as a pushover in male relationships. An additional pile on, she was raised on conditional love. When she became a Christian, Adele's tendency heightened further into God-pleasing. Perfectionism ruled most of her thoughts and how she planned her moments, days and life.

Sadly, Adele was so caught in the vortex of focusing on others first she had completely abandoned her own identity. Staring into the mirror, she didn't recognize the person reflected before her.

The confusion about who she really was overwhelmed her. In a state of complete unknowingness, yet realizing she needed to find this person once again, she sought counseling.

The counselor Adele hired called her on "her stuff," and this reality check began her slow stirring of consciousness. This was one of many a-ha clues that would lead Adele from her state of numbness into the state of awareness needed to drive change.

One obvious clue to Adele's crisis was that she answered questions on the counseling assessment as though they were for her husband, Chris. He was front and center again, instead of her. This was further proof of her lost cause for self-preservation.

Adele slowly started to awake after 15 years of being in a relationship of betrayal, addiction and extreme attachment. This awakening for Adele had taken the form of Rip Van Winkle. But instead of 100 years, in total it took ten. All of the time during her slumber, Adele dreamt that somehow she could find the secret sauce to becoming the perfect wife. Being perfect was her goal – being as sensually perfect as all of the porn models that lured Chris into late night visual ecstasy, as physically perfect as a mom of four could be through extreme workouts and dieting and as emotionally perfect as the answer to Chris' every emotional deficit and needs as a man.

Adele was excellent in all of this and more – but never perfect.

Concurrent with her therapy, she mustered the courage to confront her parents for their role in her situation. They didn't fully understand or face their faults, as they were part of the complicated web that groomed her to this place. But at their core, they loved Adele. They supported and encouraged her to continue to get the help she needed.

Adele was still convinced there was no way out. The church had her trapped with their teachings. Two confidantes she thought were friends tried to micromanage her thoughts and actions to make sure she was staying spiritual enough.

And Chris? He continued to imprint in Adele's mind that his behavior was not bad, and by the way, according to him she wasn't even good enough for another man.

The pain and tug of war with who she was and wasn't almost came to a grinding halt. Adele was ready to end all of the pain. She even had a place and a plan – both allowing her the perfect opportunity to permanently stop the madness. This act for certain would be perfect even when she couldn't be.

While laying out the details of plan execution, she came across a question that pierced her soul like the beam of a taser. "Do you believe the world is better off with or without you?" The question jumped off the page.

While pondering the question, Adele knew she had to abandon her intention. She fortunately knew the world definitively was not better off without her. If no one else needed her, her kids did. So instead of creating a plan to die, Adele started designing a purpose to live.

Over this 10-year period of coming out, Adele poured countless amounts of sweat equity into herself while at the same time still trying to appease her Chris. Finally, after reading the book "Boundaries" by

Cloud and Townsend, it was as though a beaming light shone brighter than ever on her drowsy face.

Adele learned she was *"responsible to but not for"* Chris. For the first time she was brutally honest with him and declared her truth. "This is what I need if I'm going to be available to you," she boldly claimed. She finally told Chris they would separate if he looked at pornography again. To no one's surprise, he did.

> *The awareness that we have choices can be transforming and ultimately life changing.*

For six long months of separation, Adele continued her journey into self-discovery. She finally realized she had choices. She reports today the recognition of having options and choices was what changed her approach and ultimately "changed her (my) life." She knew she wasn't trapped unless she chose to be.

While on her scavenger hunt for tools that would help her escape the trap, she also came across the work "Attached" by Amir Levine. Adele realized she suffered from attachment disorder.

As a voracious learner, Adele started combing through mounds of material on sex addiction, attachment and narcissism. She became a student of the tricks of manipulation and control she had played into for all of those years. This newfound knowledge was exactly what she needed to understand and sharpen her mind, only to realize her condition was going to stay the same if she stayed in the same relationship.

During the six-month separation and throughout her journey, Adele begged Chris to get help. He was still convinced of his innocence and worked to persuade her that every normal man wanted to revel in lustful pursuit of scintillating entertainment. He tried to justify his addiction – over and over again. Yet at times he conceded to her wish for him to stop. It wasn't escapable for Chris because he was in a trap of his own. And in reality, he didn't want to get out. For him, it was a long-desired adventure.

With Adele's adjusted norm and fresh perspective, she knew the marriage wasn't sustainable. At some point, she would need to become a teacher to her kids, her friends and the world around her about the kind of authentic woman she had become.

Once again, Adele went back in for another round. Chris convinced her he would change.

Adele and Chris had a large house with additional room to spare, so any friends or family in need of temporary housing were always in and out. This revolving door of distraction often provided the desired diversion from issues that needed to be reconciled between the two of them. It was much easier than having to face the reality of their never-ending desperate and hopeless dance.

Shortly after Adele moved back in, one of Chris' friends, David, with his wife Cheri, moved in for six months while their dream home was being built. During this time, Adele would unknowingly be given the perfect code for escaping her trap.

Operating in his typical modus operandi, Chris had a motive for his hospitable gesture. As a calculating master of life's chessboard, he had schemed a move he was confident would trap Adele for good. But his plan backfired.

One night after a few drinks, Chris purposefully confessed to David that he was simultaneously in two affairs. He knew this would anger David and in some strange way even nudge him toward pursuing Adele himself. David always praised Adele for having it all together – beauty, brains, personality. And Chris was right about his first move. David fell for it.

David started playing into Adele's needs around the house. He fixed the broken sink, installed a pencil sharpener for the kids, and offered any other act of service he thought would bring him attention and praise. Adele noticed it and admittedly started liking it. It felt good to be attended to without an expectation of reciprocation. All the things Chris's busy schedule as a doctor and addict didn't allow him to do, David was giving to her. She confessed her gradual attraction for David to her friends.

Instead of encouraging Adele to stay the course and create boundaries, they started critiquing her Christianity. They micromanaged her to the extent they would check her texts and phone lists – just to make sure she wasn't succumbing to the temptation of David's outpouring of attention.

One day when Adele was talking to David in the kitchen while everyone else was away, he told her about Chris's two affairs in the hope she would run into his arms. Adele's heartbeat quickened as her mind rewound to all the scenes from their relationship and the hurt she had endured. The curtain suddenly opened and Chris's never-ending deceit lay before her.

This was it. The final moment of truth and the revelation needed for her to escape. An unprecedented feeling of anger translated into empowerment. She was now ready to fight for herself versus a marriage that wasn't worth saving.

She screamed in delight, "I am enough!" *Thank you for ironically teaching me this truth* she whispered inside her head in gratitude to Chris. His actions had set her free for her final move. This was Adele's game and life board to play. Checkmate.

Overcoming the Excuse Ruse

It is uncanny how we rationalize in our procrastination to escape. Donna was sure she would pull the trigger after she painted the house she shared with George. She planned to live in the house after she mustered up the courage for divorce.

And Madison was sure she would do "it" after she got the last of three kids through high school.

Marcie wanted to get her varicose veins fixed before moving forward with divorce. The list of rationalizations for staying connected is endless. And retrospectively for all, ridiculous at best.

All the while, continuing to enable the trapper and convincing ourselves and the trapper that it's okay. We're encouraging and teasing the trapper. We are deceiving them and ourselves into thinking it will get better. Those few moments of masqueraded happiness with the kids or the partner or spouse sustain us. Or we let the pending sense of completion, false hope and fake joy associated with the must-get-the-house painted box checked, keep us in the cell.

> *We have to honor our own truth versus the truth of others as our guide.*

Once we reveal our truth to others, depending on their truth, they may also add to and support staying in the relationship. "Julie's husband changed, so can Chris," was a frequent intended message of hope to Adele from one of her friends.

Her parents chimed in with their doubt, "How will you support yourself and the kids?" While her own internal critical parent screamed within her, "Are you sure you've done your best and given it your all?"

That's why we have to honor our own truth, because others are continually feeding their truth into us. We can't trust THEIR truth to be OUR guide for our lives or be the recipe for our mental and emotional health and happiness.

What about the Christian or spiritual worldview or perspective? Many argue marriage wasn't designed for happiness. But rather, it was created to perfect us, make us holy or teach us how to conflict with those we love. Yes, marriage *can* do all those things.

In this worldview, the first marriage was pre-destined between Adam and Eve. Adam was already perfect. He was already holy and two perfect people would not know or be introduced into a conflictive situation. What was to perfect?

My personal belief is this marriage myth is a lie. Who knows where it originated? My hunch is it was crafted by a legalistic person who probably was not happy in her own marriage, but had an extra helping of holiness in telling the rest of us to wallow in abuse and subsequent misery.

In "The Holy Bible," the book of Deuteronomy speaks of how the Hebrew man should take a year off work for the purpose of investing in his marriage for the happiness of his wife.

"...For one year he is to be free to stay at home and bring happiness to the wife he has married." ~ NIV
"...He shall be free at home one year and shall give happiness to his wife whom he has taken." ~ NAS
"...He gets one year off simply to be at home making his wife happy." ~ The Message

Perhaps an unrealistic financial scenario for most of us; however, it speaks truth about how marriage is absolutely about co-creating happiness! Somewhere I'm hearing an "Amen." Yet in another corner I'm sure there is disbelief that as a Christian I would take this road.

> *By staying in an abusive relationship, we model and set the course for how our children will be treated and treat others in their own relationships. How can a person with solid conscious intent handle this reality?*

In taking this stance, I often feel like Kevin

Bacon in the movie "Footloose," where he appeals to the town council. The small town has a law in place forbidding dancing at the high school. This is perpetuated by the town crier, a preacher who has taken spiritual oversight and leadership to a new level. Bacon uses scripture given to him by the preacher's daughter to appeal to the ultra-righteous townspeople, who continue to uphold the law of the land denying those who wish to simply dance as a form of celebration. Here is the foundation of his compelling case found in Ecclesiastes 3:1-8. He makes his point as intended; there truly is a time for everything.

"¹There is a time for everything, and a season for every activity under the heavens:² a time to be born and a time to die, a time to plant and a time to uproot,³ a time to kill and a time to heal, a time to tear down and a time to build,⁴ a time to weep and a time to laugh, a time to mourn and a time to dance,⁵a time to scatter stones and a time to gather them, a time to embrace and a time to refrain from embracing,⁶ a time to search and a time to give up, a time to keep and a time to throw away,⁷ a time to tear and a time to mend, a time to be silent and a time to speak,⁸ a time to love and a time to hate, a time for war and a time for peace."

Yes, indeed. There is a time to refrain from embracing, and a time to give up. We have to use our best discernment to decipher the timing of that moment.

Susan, from chapter one, had an invaluable prayer partner, Kelly, who herself had been through divorce. She shared the belief with Susan of God's calling in a marriage or any healthy relationship written in Ephesians 5 (NIV):

"³But among you there must not be even a hint of sexual immorality, or of any kind of impurity, or of greed, because these are improper for God's holy people. ⁴Nor should there be obscenity, foolish talk or coarse joking, which are out of place, but rather thanksgiving. ⁵For of this you can be sure: No immoral, impure or greedy person—such a person is an idolater – has any inheritance in the kingdom of Christ and of God. ⁶Let no one deceive you with empty words, for because of such things God's wrath comes on those who are disobedient. ⁷Therefore do not be partners with them.

"⁸For you were once darkness, but now you are light in the Lord. Live as children of light ⁹(for the fruit of the light consists in all goodness, righteousness and truth) ¹⁰ and find out what pleases the Lord. ¹¹ Have nothing to do with the fruitless deeds of darkness, but rather expose them. ¹² It is shameful even to mention what the disobedient do in secret. ¹³ But everything exposed by the light becomes visible – and everything that is illuminated becomes a light. ¹⁴ This is why it is said: "Wake up, sleeper, rise from the dead, and Christ will shine on you."

Susan realized she should not be married to Mike. That she should come out of the darkness in the relationship so she could regain herself and be light again.

Granted, a solid and healthy marriage may not always bring happiness. It is never another person's job to make us happy. Joyful couples are typically comprised of two individuals who are true and authentic to themselves and figure out a way to co-create happiness as a unit. They continually problem-solve a way to manage around the sticky day-to-day issues of life.

Dr. John Gottman, Founder of the Gottman Institute, leading Therapist and Researcher in the field of relationships, established strong predictors on whether or not stable couples would be happy or unhappy using measures of positive affect during conflict. Dr. Jim Coan, Associate Professor of Clinical Psychology and Director of the Virginia Affective Neuroscience Laboratory at the University of Virginia, and Dr. John Gottman both discovered these measures were not used randomly but to purposefully physiologically soothe the partner.

Dr. Gottman also discovered that in healthy relationships, men accepting influence from women was predictive of a happy and stable marriage. An additional variable of happiness was revealed by Dr. Bob Levenson's and Anna Ruef's research. In their study, humor was found to be soothing, and, in addition, the use of empathy had a positive physiological impact.

If you're not happy in a marriage due to emotional, mental, spiritual or physical abuse, you have every right to seek escape and freedom.

The truth, when properly guided, will surely set us free.

Finding Your Courage

Once we decide we are worth fighting for, how do we start the process?

Adele knew there were some things she could do well and one of them was to teach others. She had majored in education and home-schooled her children. As a first step, she would teach others how to do what she had done. She would share all her knowledge and borne-out experiences with others.

She relied on her strength of teaching other women to make herself accountable in walking out her freedom. She found a local nonprofit that empowered women to become whole again through counseling, coaching and group support. Adele signed up for a group as a way of garnering support and soon moved into giveback by teaching a group for current and former wives of sex addicts. Adele realized what others meant when they said, "The highest form of knowing is teaching others." She found hope and sustenance in helping others thrive through what she had lived.

Nancy, one of Susan's other friends, drove home the truth about what she was teaching her daughter by staying in the marriage. This would be the modeling and lesson for how her daughter should expect to be treated in her future relationships. Nancy emphatically expressed this to Susan after another verbal and physical episode with Mike, knowing her daughter witnessed the episode. This time, Susan finally heard it loud and clear. To ignore this was to ignore and abuse my daughter, she thought. Compounding this realization, lay the fact of how it was also teaching her son how to treat his future girlfriends and wife. Could she handle this in good consciousness?

Susan remembers the first time her voice started coming back. It was when she told Kelly about the abuse. Kelly had sensed Susan's need for perfection. She had noticed her sensitivity about how Mike would react to certain things, and she heard the trepidation in Susan's voice in deciding to accept an invitation for an outing. Kelly's discerning spirit knew the chains that must be in place.

When Kelly asked, "Is your marriage doing okay?" Susan broke the silence. She knew Kelly was trustworthy and had her best interests at heart, and for the first time ever, the secret was revealed. She heard out loud the harsh ugly relationship reality of her life with Mike. Her voice didn't lie. It was undeniable. She was in an abusive relationship.

It was strange to her how hearing it outside of her head made it more real.

Like Adele, this was the start of Susan realizing the power of support from other women as a critical component of self-care, preservation, and ultimate release from the trap. It was other women who would listen to her hurt, pray her through her doubts and advise her to get away for a few days to gain perspective and create a plan for her pending escape.

She found her courage through the strength of others lifting her in unimaginable ways. Soon, she had the power of momentum to break free and start anew.

Shifting Your Mindset

To truly start over, Susan needed to continue the path of a new mindset. Along with the sage advice from wise friends and a solid counselor, another friend gave her an article on "Just in Time Thinking" by Martha Beck. It was as if she saw the heavens part and the sun shine for the first time.

Driving home from that encounter with the freshly-printed article on her lap ready to be taken in by her wanting mind, the epiphany of her pattern of living in scarcity engulfed her. She had held on to a lousy relationship and life because she thought that was as good as it could get. And if she left it, what if she never ended up in a better place? The closely held idiom of, "Better the devil you know than the devil you don't know," had partially kept her tethered to mediocrity.

By living in a place of fear, Susan had forfeited many of her better, more attractive options. She now all too clearly grasped the importance of living from a place of abundance versus scarcity. Realizing what she needed had always found her and she had never gone hungry, without shelter or without the resources needed – Susan held her head high.

This previous proof of concept boosted Susan's confidence that the money, the love and anything else she had held onto with clenched fists would be restored – better than ever. Actually holding onto what she thought was good enough prevented the best of the things she deserved from finding their way to her.

Through prayer and meditation combined with faith and trust, she stopped living in a place of fear and learned about the power of desire.

About this same time, the learning continued from other teachable moments. A speaker at a workshop shared a story about a single woman who put together a dream book of pictures and phrases that paralleled with the desires of her heart and the life she truly believed she was worthy of. Over time, most of these things found that woman!

So that weekend, Susan started her own dream book and gazed longingly over each picture and concept. She carefully pasted her rendition of the life she wanted – page by hopeful page.

Upon letting the marriage go and claiming her future, miracles began to unfold all around her. The monthly program she had begun delivering and counting on as a main source of income was eliminated due to budget constraints. Why was that so good? Because she landed a client, just a couple of weeks later – her largest contract engagement ever. Over time, more business was birthed and they referred her to other clients, one of which is her biggest client today. Additional proliferation ensued. After all, her dream book visually displayed: "Have Customers Lining Up," "Climbing Revenues" and even more aspirational declarations about what was possible.

After being told for years she wasn't athletic, Susan started training and competing in triathlons. She ultimately qualified and competed in the national championship for her age group. Fortuitously, her dream book claimed "Compete in Your First Tri" and "Go the Distance" as visions that would happen. And they did.

She finally found happiness in that beautiful house that was never a home until she made it one – by filling it full of people she could love and bless with another one of her gifts of hospitality. Those pictures of entertaining stress-free, smiling and fellowshipping pasted in her dream book danced in her head each time she opened the front door. For three years in a down real estate market she made a large payment for a house that was out of her budget possibilities, without tapping savings. It just happened. She never worried.

She finally sold that house knowing there would be "the right house at the right time at the right price" (also the exact picture of the house in her dream book). The house she purchased was the same layout, but smaller, with perfect colors and the exact roses off the porch like those in the dream book. Amazing! And the move to the new place just happened to orchestrate with the move-out date of the old home.

A year later, her friend nudged her while car-shopping to go look at the last car available from that model year. She knew Susan could negotiate rock-bottom pricing. Years before, she had pasted a picture of that same car in her book, thinking it might happen near retirement after her children were raised, sent to college and on their own. It was a stretch, she thought, as the rubber cement glided over the back of it, before she secured it to the anointed page.

Why not look, Susan thought. It was just a dream and she was now free to dream what she wanted! The salesperson desperately quoted Susan an offer too good to refuse on the coveted car in her book, which was comparable to the payment on the other car she was considering. Susan bought the car.

Many more stories from Susan's life could be shared. What Susan would tell you is that almost every picture from that 30-page book became reality, because she trusted from a position of abundance versus scarcity. Her enduring faith and recaptured mindset taught her

"What the locusts have eaten would be restored," and, "More than we can hope or imagine can be provided."

As of this writing, just one page with a visual from Susan's dream book has not yet come true. It's a picture of her wedding reception, posted three years prior to meeting her fiancé. The guy in the picture even looks like her fiancé. And, as expected, they are blissfully dancing and having the time of their lives.

BREAKTHROUGH MOMENTS

- In what ways have you been in a deep trance or sleep in your relationship?

- What distractions do you keep inviting in to allow you to avoid taking the necessary steps for change?

- What nudges have you received to awake from the sleep? How have you responded? Why?

- What one thing will it take for you to see the blinding light and start to move out of the trap?

- What is your truth? What do you need to do to claim it?

- What are you teaching others about who you really are? Are you teaching that you and your heart are worth saving?

- What one boundary do you need to create and claim today?

BREAK AWAY THOUGHTS

- Timing is never perfect. Trust your truth and let it guide you to the right decision.

- People teach you who they are. Believe them.

- Would you choose your partner or spouse as a friend? If not, you shouldn't be in union with him.

- Until you stop inviting distractions into your trap, you will always be able to numb or ignore the discomfort and pain that truly exists inside the trap.

- You have to feel the pain to acknowledge it and act on it. Let yourself feel it.

RESOURCES

"Journal of Personality and Social Psychology," Vol 63(2), Aug 1992, 234-246.http://dx.doi.org/10.1037/0022-3514.63.2.234

https://www.gottman.com/about/research/couples/

~CHAPTER FIVE~

KNOW WHO YOU ARE AND WHAT YOU WANT

The Head versus the Heart

To make sense of the never-ending song of the irrational, Meriam repeatedly rationalized what seemed so out of tune. How could Craig be so calm and steady at certain times and so volatile during others? The unpredictability was maddening. It was like walking on eggshells. Craig's unanticipated reaction was always lurking like a monster in the closet ready to jump out at any moment.

Meriam worked harder than ever to keep peace. She meticulously calculated having dinner done on time just as Craig liked it – perfectly timed like an orchestral production. At all costs, Meriam tried to never repeat the episode where Craig exploded because the side items weren't finished in perfect concert with the grilled steaks. Keeping Craig's disappointment to a quasi-predictable level that avoided escalation to anger was always a goal.

The details were etched in Meriam's mind forever, so she didn't have to work to recall them vividly. This day was like many with four kids and the erratic uncertain behavior that could erupt. Soccer games, a sick child, and the typical Saturday chores and errands presented the usual line up. In playing the "What's for dinner?" game, Meriam didn't have time or the luxury to be tired or to consider bringing in take out. It was another requisite gourmet meal night at the Moore's.

During preparation, Craig talked with Meriam through every detail tied to the timing of the meal. She would get it right. No excuses.

However when Craig entered with the steaks and announced they were done, Meriam hadn't kept her end of the culinary bargain. She had gotten sidetracked giving their squeamish four year-old medicine while wiping tears from the six year-old's face, whose untimely skating accident left her knee scraped and requiring a bandage.

Just five minutes more and dinner would have been ready. That wasn't good enough for Craig whose steak was growing cold. This wasn't the first time his anger spilled over into what seemed to be a trivial issue for Meriam. But to Craig, perfect timing was tantamount.

After feeling the piercing, verbal lashing from Craig for the minutes that seemed like hours, Meriam lost control. She tossed Craig's potato to him with his back turned and issued a simple, late warning of, "Here you go! Here's your potato!" After all, she thought, Craig so desperately wanted the potatoes on the table and that was the only thing holding up his dinner. The intended toss might also send the message of her growing hurt and anger over Craig's continued disappointing reminders about her not having a dinner item ready precisely on his timeline.

With an unexpected shove from behind, Meriam felt her side hip forcefully slide into the granite island. Quickly gaining her composure with the kids in close tow, she pretended it didn't happen.

Unfortunately, this was not the last time it happened. It was one of many sporadic episodes that would continue over the years, just another blatant reason for Meriam to leave. What was keeping her in this place?

Meriam's mind shifted to the time her ten year-old daughter climbed into the SUV with her. Immediately after witnessing her dad give Meriam mean-spirited marching orders through the half rolled-down window about how and when to pick up his pharmacy items, her daughter knew the truth. Within moments, Meriam's daughter both innocently and demonstratively shared her observation, "Mommy, Daddy doesn't have any idea how mean he treats you!"

Maybe he does or maybe he doesn't, Meriam wanted to say. Either way Meriam knew it wasn't okay, and now a ten year-old observer was validating what she wanted to believe and confirmed where it mattered most – deep down inside herself.

More messaging from the children continued as the behavior cropped up episodically. A few months later, Meriam made the all-too familiar turn into the neighborhood with the unknowing, sinking feeling in the pit of her stomach on how she would be greeted. Thinking out loud, the words unintentionally left her brain and went through her mouth, "I wonder what kind of mood your Dad will be in today?"

The often internalized question was now spoken into the ears of Meriam's 13 year-old son. Without hesitation his wise young soul mentored her, "Mom, if you have to ask yourself that question each time you come into the neighborhood, that tells you something, doesn't it?"

Indeed it does, son, Meriam thought without replying, yet screaming it inside her head.

Getting the Head and Heart Aligned

Some would argue the heart is the lanyard with its strings keeping us tied to broken relationships. They would say it is the part that is always behind the head to succumb to the necessary action of doing the right thing. This was not so with Meriam's experience.

Meriam's heart left the relationship many years before she could rationalize her eventual actions to end the relationship. It was her heart that would keep her awake at night fighting to tear the chains of a desperately wrong situation. Her heart knew the way but her head would not believe it and follow.

The head, the logical part of our brains, always wants to help us rationalize why we should stay. It is fighting for every bit of compelling reasoning that suggests we need to work it out, endure, and even continue to trap us in the revolving door problem-solving that convinces us it will get better.

Rational thinking is fear-based and fear is ALWAYS a limiting force. When operating in a fearful mindset, we close our minds and then consequently numb our hearts to options. It can be paralyzing and usually is.

Listen to your heart and sixth sense more than your head. The direction it takes you is invariably the right one.

The heart, on the other hand, will show us the path to take and be our faithful guide if we will slow down enough to listen and follow. When we're busy, we cannot hear our hearts speaking to us. When we eliminate the noise around us, we can hear the beat of the drum and our innermost soul is the drummer who calls us to our best place – if only we will listen. Unlike the head, the heart can take us to a place of desire even in the worst situations.

Desire is the birthplace of abundance that was mentioned in chapter four. We have to know there will always be enough. Trusting the process and letting go are imperative to the extent we may not yet see the desired state in the beginning, but know over time it will be revealed to us. That is the manifestation of faith, "Being sure of what we hope for and certain of what we do not see" (The Holy Bible, Hebrews 11:1).

Reclaiming You and Your Worth

The Value of Values

Socrates said, "Know Thyself." A common thread among all the women caught in the trap is a momentary loss of identity. Their true selves are still tucked inside; they just have to find themselves again and give permission to come out.

At every person's core and identity are the values that navigate every behavior every moment of every day. These are called core values and are the true north against which every action has to be measured.

What are your values? Do you know what is most important to you? Mine are faith, family and health. Many women I know are hardwired to answer, "Family!" Depending on innate personality types, along with how we're nurtured, the expression of values can vary for each of us.

We're going to dissect the values proposition more in a few moments, but it is certainly easy to see how our DNA-encoded value of family can prevent us from taking the very action that would break apart our definition of that family.

Knowing and claiming your values provides an internal compass that will help you figure out every decision and behavior for the rest of your life.

A list of values and an activity are available at the end of this chapter. Ask yourself:

- What do I care most about? What am I willing to fight for or defend?
- What are my non-negotiables? Things I absolutely will not give up for anything else – regardless of the price?

- When I look at where I spend my money and allocate my time, what does it reveal about what is most important to me?

Are you living your values? Are any of your values preventing you from honoring your truest and best self?

Having values as an anchor, you can expand your intention of claiming who you are by knowing your vision and your mission for life. What is your desired state? Who are you at your innermost being and how does that translate into who you want to be? A vision statement does just that. It helps you envision your aspirational state of being. It defines who you want to be at your highest and best place. Many businesses use a vision statement to guide them to their desired state. It keeps their "eyes on the prize" so to speak and gives them hope and promise for the success and direction of the future.

An example follows:

My vision is a family and life where we are all contributing and living out our full potential by using our gifts to influence our current and future direction.

After much research on personal vision and mission statements, Meriam landed on the following vision for herself: To live in complete authenticity and create a defining legacy of positive impact on my family and all those I love.

Both vision and mission statements should be concise, inspirational and memorable. While vision is focused on the ideal future state, mission is about the ideal current state of how we walk out our intention daily. It is what we do, our purpose in life that defines who we epitomize and what we do moment by moment.

Meriam crafted her mission as, "To live in truth every day and be at my best and brightest place loving and serving those I love and respect."

Take a hard look at who you are as a woman and as a person. What is your vision for what you are aspiring to become? What is your purpose or mission daily?

Pursue and Enlist the Necessary Resources

While seeking these answers from within, Meriam also gained the help of caring women who supported her in prayer and advice. She met with a prayer group of three women weekly who invested in her through encouragement, Godly counsel and prayer time.

Meriam kept seeking input from multiple sources and attended an experience called *Focus Seminars of Kansas City* (www.focusseminar.com). Focus is a professional organization that invites all to conquer life's challenges and move toward new levels of personal growth. As part of their premier offering, attendees go through an intensive three weekend session about discovering who they really are at their most true self so they can reclaim it.

In three weekends over a six-week period, Meriam discovered new insights, a sense of community with other seekers and most importantly, she found and reclaimed herself. During this process, Meriam, along with the other attendees, worked through stages of learning that allowed each of them to create a contract with themselves about who they really were, not the mask they had all learned to wear so comfortably in an effort to please others.

Meriam put a stake in the ground, and by the second weekend, she knew who she was in her heart – playful, authentic and worthy. This would be the litmus test by which she could now judge all her actions. Was she showing up as any of these in her relationship with Craig? No.

Would he "allow" her to? And most importantly, would she allow herself? That was the big question.

Meriam took a required oath at the beginning of the seminar not to make any relationship changes either during the seminar or in the 90 days after the program was over. She knew this meant she would need an extension of assistance to keep her true to her contract and to help her navigate many decisions that lay ahead.

Meriam met a trainer in the Focus Program she sought out as a counselor. This wise individual could relate exceptionally and soulfully well to Meriam, as she herself had been caught in the trap and divorced a few years prior. She had walked this familiar road. In using her professional prowess and intuition, she could completely relate to and assist Meriam in her need for a plan of escape.

She would be an essential piece of the puzzle in helping Meriam find that step out of the head fog and connect to her heart's desire. She would be the one that would evoke Merriam to reveal and claim the phrase, "I love options." Now armed with the awareness of having options, Merriam could express her affinity for owning them. And through a well-played out and in many respects fortuitous process, for the first time ever, she would learn she had many paths she could potentially take. Knowing this gave Meriam much of the energy she would need in the coming months.

The Power of Personal Conquests

Diane had always been competitive. She had possessed a strong drive and adventuresome spirit as long as she could remember. Raised around mostly boy cousins, she wouldn't be outdone in tree climbing contests. While staying with her grandmother during her preschool years, her favorite go-to playmate was a neighbor boy she would constantly challenge to barefoot runs on the gravel roads of the rural countryside around her grandmother's farm.

In elementary school at recess, while other girls were jumping rope, Diane could be found on the basketball court shooting hoops with the boys and one other "tomboy" from her class. Diane didn't try to be different, a "one-upsman" or overly-competitive, it was simply part of her hardwiring.

Focusing on a personal conquest or something just for you will keep you centered and make you stronger to face the bigger challenges ahead.

It was this tough, rugged spirit and determination that would take her through the final leg of her escape from Chad. Diane was angry, very angry. Instead of using it negatively, she used it to bolster herself in readying for the anticipated rough ride ahead.

Even before making the final break from her trap, she hired a personal trainer. It was through these sessions that she would engender the physical strength that in many ways empowered her mentally for her escape. Her trainer would often remark that she had the raw determination to take on any challenge many of his male clients couldn't muster. Diane knew her secret sauce. But her trainer was in the dark regarding this unidentifiable push that drove her to master each and every workout.

A few months after working out together, Diane's trainer noticed a large black and blue bruise on her left forearm, stretching from the bottom of her hand all the way to her elbow. When he asked her what happened, Diane cleverly claimed she fell on the ice a few days before. How fortunate for Diane that it was February and the weather had been her scapegoat for Chad's squeezing force during a struggle in the kitchen a few nights prior. Her trainer didn't drill down for more information. Telling these little white lies that had become so familiar to Diane in allowing her to hide the real relationship secrets from her friends and family, and she now hid the truth from her trainer as well.

While Diane was telling lies, Chad was working on his own myths. He explained the problem to Diane by telling her that she bruised much too easily and she must have a health problem. Yes, Diane did bruise easily, yet she knew it was Chad's unyielding force in pushing her from the kitchen to the laundry room with an absolute death grip on her arm that led to this colorful masquerade.

Weekly gaining physical strength, Diane was able to think more clearly and gain mental stamina. As she continued to learn about what she wanted, she decided to take on a personal conquest. How could she take all of the competitiveness she had hardwired inside, stir it with some of her newfound physical strength, and mix it up to gain much-needed confidence to reinstate her belief in herself?

Through a series of encounters, she was led to competing in half marathons. This gave Diane the think time needed to process her next steps in her breakaway, while allowing her to express her desired freedom through running. Over time, this would symbolically represent Diane's ability to gain the necessary momentum to start going and keep going in leaping the steps to her destiny of breaking free.

For Tonya, who had gone through her release process a few years before, it was a different outlet and outlook, but she accomplished the same goal. She had decided to do the one thing she feared the most — scuba diving. Tonya first learned how to swim at the high school pool while taking lessons from a generous friend who was a lifeguard and swim team champion in school.

After checking on this first necessary step, she saved enough money to take scuba lessons and become certified. It would be a couple of years later with her newfound freedom that she would be able to go on a scuba diving trip and meet the man her heart had been longing for. Tonya's courage helped her gain a new skill that led her to a new hobby, which eventually led her to whom she would later describe as her soul mate.

Both Diane and Tonya used their personal interests, desires and even fears as a winning formula for gaining the mental, physical and emotional strength to make their escape.

Not everyone can or needs to do this through a half marathon or scuba diving. The punch line is to look at what you do best or have always wanted to do – and then to conquer it.

BREAKTHROUGH MOMENTS

- Below is a list of potential values. What are your top 3-5 values? Check them off.

Examples of Personal Core Values:

o   Achievement
o   Adventure
o   Affection
o   Variety
o   Relationships
o   Integrity
o   Self-respect
o   Knowledge
o   Personal Growth
o   Status
o   Personal growth
o   Family
o   Physical challenges
o   Helping Others
o   Community Service and Impact
o   Meaningful work
o   Finances
o   Recognition
o   Stability
o   Creative Expression
o   Time
o   Other_____
o   Other_____

- In what ways are these values aligned with your heart? How will you follow your heart and not let your head get in the way of following your core values?

- Using the guidelines and examples in this chapter, what is your vision for your future? What is your purpose and mission you would like to live daily?

  My Vision or Desired/Ideal State is:

  My Mission or Current State/Daily Purpose is:

- What one resource can you contact today to help you get to the next step?

- What is the legacy you want to create and live?

- How is staying in your current situation preventing you from creating the best legacy you are capable of – for yourself? For your family?

BREAK AWAY THOUGHTS

- Spend time in journaling, prayer and meditation daily so you can hear the beat of your heart and Spirit. He always knows the way. Trust and follow.

- You are stronger than you know. Remember who you are. When you are living your values, mission and vision you will operate from a place of strength.

- Keep perspective and stay resilient – any current pain or discomfort is temporary. When your head and heart become aligned, you will begin to experience a feeling of expression and self-integrity that is unparalleled. It is worth the pain to get there.

RESOURCES

http://askmehouse.com/community/vlrc/resolved-to-change-align-head-and-heart/

http://www.simplemindfulness.com/2012/03/17/head-vs-heart-which-is-smarter/

~CHAPTER SIX~

ENVISION AND PLAN YOUR STRATEGY

A Change of Scenery for Clarity

It was two months into her weekly gathering with the women who had surrounded, supported and prayed for her, that a new revelation came. "What if you got away for a couple of days, Karla?" asked her friend and comrade who had walked with her through this storm.

Karla squelched her momentary excitement with reality. How could she possibly leave the kids for a weekend with so many loose ends untied right now? It seemed too good to be true. Two days away? Alone? Where would she go? What would she do?

> *A way of escape – somehow, someway – will always come. Keeping your mind open to the possibilities and timing is what will make it reality.*

Before her mind wandered too much, the group intervened, "You need a quiet place, not too far away, where you can just relax, do some journaling and clear your head."

Another friend quickly joined in, "I know someone with a place on the lake about 30 minutes from here. My friend isn't going there much these days, so I bet she would let you stay there next weekend." The excitement filled the cozy room around the ottoman where they had met, shared their innermost hearts, read encouraging truths and prayed for the past eight weeks.

Everything else had fallen into place and Karla knew this idea was spirit-breathed. She decided without question after the group's moments of inspiration to tell Paul she needed to get away for the weekend. As an extra measure, she would have a sitter on-call and close by, just in case Paul said "No" to watching the kids.

As almost guaranteed, the friend with the lake home was more than happy to allow Karla to use her lake getaway for the weekend. With great trepidation, Karla couldn't help but wonder – how would she fill her time? What would it be like to just be and let her guard down? What might her heart reveal? Would she like the answer she heard? And more importantly, would she be able to embrace the revelation and take action?

The past year of separation had taken its toll on Karla. She had so desperately wanted Paul to step up, show a regretful and contrite heart and more importantly show her he was willing to change. However, that was far from what had unfolded. Paul continued drinking excessively, refused marital counseling beyond the first session and insisted he didn't have a problem. In fact, he was still trying to convince Karla that *she* was the problem.

Karla didn't deny she had flaws and could always improve. Yet she knew in her heart and her head that Paul was still the spoiled little boy his doting mother had raised. Growing up, he had been lavishly praised in spite of anything he did wrong and now was manifesting as a narcissist. She had observed it as early as their first month of marriage, researched it, lived it and at this point had suffered through it for years. It was enough for any good or not so good woman to endure.

In spite of the addiction, abuse and unhappiness, Karla felt torn about cutting the final cord. In many ways it was as though she had all but unraveled from the ball of thread that had wrapped around her entire being. She had known about the inherent flaws to the relationship's fabric. Even with this blaring truth, it was as though she couldn't keep from making the next clockwise turn that placed another winding thread of commitment around her tiny frame and big heart.

Just one year ago, after more than a dozen painful years, Karla had finally filed for divorce. Five years before, she had awakened and knew the charade was destined for demise. It was like a blighted hope – so much potential and promise – but just enough toxic poison that religion, regular date nights and the required relationship prerequisite of love – for better or for worse – couldn't serve as the antidote to make it right.

Karla had to make a decision. One year into separation and the divorce circus had left her depressed, lethargic and indecisive. She had given Paul too much time – so much that he had regained his senses after the shock of the filing. He had rounded up a bulldog attorney and was in for the fight. Ironically all the while saying he wanted to make it work, yet he was unwilling and perhaps even unable to make the true change needed for a healthy, functioning relationship.

In her mind, this was her final stop. Either she would go at full speed forward or resign herself to seven more years of misery. This would carry her to the end of the last child's graduation from high school, providing a logical choice to the road before her. This was the road most selected and traveled by others in her shoes.

Karla knew what she had to do. Like everything else she put her mind to, she made the lake getaway happen. Paul agreed to watch the two younger kids while the oldest was away with a friend. The homeowner agreed to meet Karla the day before her departure to pass off the keys. Could it be this easy? In less than 24 hours, she would have two days to herself for the first time in ages. Instead of focusing on what she would do, her thoughts quickly shifted to what she would discover about herself – things she wanted to know and maybe – those she didn't.

It was a sunny yet cool fall day, and Karla awoke with great anticipation in her heart. She mapped out her 35-minute drive to the rural lake setting just outside the city. Her excitement intensified as she drove along the country roads with the first signs of fall just starting to unfold. The colors energized her. The more she drove away from the place she had felt trapped, the more freedom she experienced.

Karla arrived at lunch time. Before satisfying the gradual knowing in her stomach, she took some time to acquaint herself with her home for the next two days. Two levels of cozy and quaint cottage met the criteria for get away and relaxation. The outside deck, a welcoming 75 degrees, furnished with comfortable chaise lounges and overlooking the lake was the perfect answer to outdoor serenity.

Karla quickly took her bags in the master bedroom then felt herself skip into the kitchen to put her food away. She had decided there would be no leaving the premises except for morning or evening walks, so like a prepared scout headed for a camping adventure she brought everything she needed. Soon Karla found her way back out to the serene outdoors, onto a chaise lounge for a long nap.

What you hear when there is silence is what you are searching for. Is it peace? Is it contentment? Does it feel different? That's when you know you want to not just go there. You need to move there. And stay. THIS is what life is supposed to be like.

Awaking refreshed and worry-free for the time being, Karla picked up her journal and began to write her feelings. While she had journaled early on in the divorce process at the prompting of her counselor, she hadn't taken the time to focus on the rigor consistently enough. It was time to claim what she wanted for her future, and the blank canvas lay before her, ready to be painted with her deepest thoughts. Karla began to script her deepest feelings about the life she wanted. She pressed into her soul's longing and was beginning to see a glimmer of hope she hadn't seen since she marched into the attorney's office to file for divorce.

As daylight began to shift to darkness with the setting sun, Karla went inside to fix herself a salad and sandwich. She didn't need more than that. While she had grown accustomed to having to prepare much more complex and lavish dinners, her modest upbringing and who she was at her core could do with much less. Was she willing to make this and the other sacrifices that would be required? In less than 48 hours she would have her answer.

Karla decided she would end her day with some nighttime viewing from one of the two large screen TVs that were a prominent part of both levels. First, she went downstairs hoping to relax on what appeared to be the more comfy of the two sofas, opting for the lower level. With remote in hand, she pushed the "On" button in anticipation of a mindless getaway before turning in for the evening. The TV would turn on, but wouldn't show a picture. She tried her technical wizardry on the remote and cable box for a few moments, and then quickly retreated to the upstairs TV. The same thing happened there.

After a while, Karla gave up and realized that perhaps she wasn't supposed to watch TV or do anything else for that matter. She came to the lake for answers, and the best answers required listening. How would she hear that inner voice if the house was filled with noise? In that moment, Karla resigned herself to silence. It would turn out to be one of the best sentences she had been given while in her personal prison, ultimately making her overall stay shorter than intended.

Karla poured more words onto paper. She picked up the Bible she brought that she recently and more frequently turned to for solace, wisdom and comfort. While reading, she fell asleep and awoke the next morning to her first full day of adventure.

The morning dew danced on the grass. While wandering on the deck, the sounds of the morning fell easily on the calm lake, a sure sign of things to come. Karla quickly dressed and her new energy forced her outside to take a walk on the country roads. With the call of birds and a soft breeze blowing through the leaves, Karla couldn't remember a walk so peaceful and relaxing.

Back at the house and after a light breakfast, Karla found herself boomeranged on to what was quickly becoming her favorite hangout on the premises – the deck. What was it about overlooking the water that calmed the soul? While Karla had never spent much time on a lake, she had spent much of her youth at the beach and had acquired an affinity for water. The echo of the ripples comforted her and took her back to a more innocent time. She thought about how she had envisioned her promise-filled life as a young girl although that vision had not come to pass.

Karla had put her cell phone on silent. She had no internet connectivity and had promised herself she would only answer the phone in the event of a family call. She left her phone in the kitchen most of the time, but in a moment of forgetfulness to her commitment, she had brought it outside.

Mid-morning, she noticed three calls from Paul. Glancing down, she saw a fourth call coming through. Reluctantly, she answered. Paul wanted to know how she was doing, and then quickly moved on to his agenda. "I need to borrow your SUV to go get the aerator I rented for the lawn." Then he boldly asked, "Can you be back a little early?"

Really! My one opportunity to get away and you can't plan around it? The resentment in Karla swelled, as she recounted the many times she had moved the chess pieces on her work calendar and kids' schedules to accommodate Paul's never-ending travel and personal requests.

"No, I can't make it back. I won't be finished or ready in time," she quickly responded.

"Why?," quipped Paul. "You don't have a set schedule, do you?"

"Yes, in fact I do," Karla forced without hesitation. "I have a long appointment tomorrow morning." And she did indeed. On the deck. In the chair. It was a three-way call – between herself, her journal and her Soul Whisperer. It might be one of the most important meetings of her life, and she didn't dare miss it.

Exasperated, Paul hung up.

He would figure it out, Karla surmised.

To get back into the moment, Karla lay in the chair, allowing her mind to think, to go inside herself and listen to her heart. The day lapsed quickly between napping and journaling. While Karla wasn't sure why, she felt compelled to leave the house for dinner that night. About 10 minutes away there was a charming Italian restaurant she had been to with a friend years before. A hearty meal might be in order. Karla hadn't attended to food for 30 hours, focused instead on feeding her soul. In the last few months her already slender body had lost more weight as the stress of the divorce seemed to melt away pounds.

Karla threw on a change of clothes and drove into town. It was early with just a few couples in the restaurant. What she noticed was worth the trip and explained why she felt the tug to be there. As she glanced at the faces, she was struck by how content they looked, how they were engaged in each other and in conversation, the antithesis of what she usually experienced with Paul.

After a plate of piping hot and filling lasagna, she finished her meal with tiramisu and took leftovers for the following day. To keep herself focused on her purpose for the getaway, Karla ignored the quaint antique stores and other potential distractions in town. She wanted to get back to the deck in time for the last hour of daylight.

Karla went to bed that night with no more answers than when she arrived, yet with a peace she hadn't known in years. She knew with certainty that the sun would rise and she would wake with the promise of what she came to find. Even though the anticipation overwhelmed her, she was quick to fall into a deep sleep, inhaling the respite her body and mind needed.

As the sun peeked through the blinds, Karla awoke to another beautiful day. She jumped out of bed and quickly went to the kitchen to make a cup of coffee for her last morning. The chaise and deck greeted her almost as though she was a desired and much-welcomed guest. *Good morning*, she wanted to shout. *I'm back to enjoy your gifts of my new day and breathe in some answers*. Without thinking, Karla grabbed her Bible, journal and pen. She hurriedly turned to the Psalms. How it resonated with her pain and suffering, just as David had sung out his cry to God at the end of his persecution.

Just like David, Karla knew her enemies would be justly dealt with and shut down. While some called it Karma, yet others referred to it as poetic justice or judgment. It didn't matter to Karla what it was called or how it would happen. She knew it would come. She didn't have to worry about when. Just the self-assurance that she was protected no matter what would lift her spirit and keep her going.

With a thirst that needed quenching, Karla turned to Psalm 143, the earnest appeal for guidance and deliverance. She penned the entire passage into her journal. As she ferociously wrote, revelation pounced on the moment. The clarity was consuming. Certainty washed over her like a rushing waterfall. She was absolutely sure about what she needed to do, and she was ready to take the next steps. What happened in that place, in that moment, perhaps wasn't explainable. She just knew she was ready for such a time as this.

Winning Takes a Team – Recruit from the Outside

Even with the proper self-work, conditioning and eventual landing upon the readiness to break away, rarely can someone finish the fight for freedom alone. Case in point: the ages old example of David and Goliath. Or the Hollywood heroic feats of Rambo taking on the military fight against an entire Vietnamese troop. Something within us loves seeing how the underdog forges ahead, especially in the face of being outnumbered. Yet, the reality is that it is more important than ever to surround yourself with a strong team.

We huddled in the previous chapter on the power of knowing who you are and claiming your values, vision and mission. We talked about taking on a personal feat or conquest to build confidence. We stated the importance of taking care of ourselves through exercise, both to channel anger and to build strength for the escape. Surrounding yourself with a support team of cheerleaders, prayer warriors and/or encouragers has also been driven home. What we haven't emphasized yet is the power of the legal and other formal counsel you select.

One of the first steps is to get input from an experienced and wise attorney. Interview at least three and ask each one these tough questions:

1- What is your track record for "winning" cases?
2- How many divorce cases have you handled?
3- How do you define success in divorce?
4- Have you personally experienced divorce?
5- What drew you into family law?
6- How much longer do you plan to practice law?
7- What is the average cost of a case like the one I've described?
8- What are the three things your former and current clients say about you and your work?
9- How will I know you have my best interests at heart versus making it about more billable hours?
10- Describe your style when you encounter opposition and resistance from the spouse's attorney? How will you work to maintain and keep our power throughout the process?

While this list isn't exhaustive, it will give insight into the attorney's style and client-centricity. Diane used three attorneys before it was all said and done. Attorney number one decided to move from family law to elder law five months into her case. If Diane had asked question number six above, this wouldn't have been an issue. She would have selected another attorney or made sure she moved the case along more quickly.

The second attorney billed hours for every time she thought about Diane's case. While claiming to be collaborative, Diane quickly learned collaboration was impossible with a manipulative narcissist. As desirable as a "hold hands and sing Kum-ba-ya" scenario sounded, it wasn't possible to be collaborative in her situation.

Attorney number three ended up representing Diane, but he wasn't as tough as Diane needed for the opposing bulldog. He allowed the other attorney to offend and intimidate him. Because he tended to operate at an emotional level, he missed some things the other attorney changed in the agreement, setting Diane up for some unnecessary financial losses.

Have a referral or two as resources, preferably both clients and other attorneys who have worked with the attorney, as a way to validate the answers you are given in the selection process.

Here are three simple criteria for choosing the right attorney:

1- **First, know what's important to you.** Before you do any outside research, look inward first and foremost. Your goal should be to get divorced – yet in the process, to protect your children's best interests and your assets – while moving through the process as quickly as possible.

   Too many people get focused on being right and lose sight of the bigger goal. Delaying the process not only costs more in emotional energy, time and financial resources, but it gives the trapper more time to come out of his daze and realize you are finally freeing yourself. The longer you wait, the higher the stakes become and the more you stand to lose in money and sweat equity.

   Can you use a court-appointed mediator? If so, that will be the least expensive route. In Diane's case, if your spouse needs to win at all costs, is in revenge mode, or is resisting the divorce, then a mediator approach will most likely not work.

Remember this is no longer personal, it's business. As in any negotiation, write down your ideal outcome and also your bottom line. Going through this exercise up front can prevent you from getting too emotional during the process when you most need your objectivity. You may need to make adjustments along the way, but it's more the case than the exception that we tend to end up with what we claim. Your actions will align with the intended result.

2- **Do your due diligence.** What is the word on the street about this attorney? Which attorney have others used? What did they like or dislike? Find at least two or preferably three attorneys to interview. Talk with them first by phone to get a sense of their style and to ask the above questions. If they make guarantees, skirt around issues or start name-dropping, move on.

3- **Set and manage expectations.** Do they talk your values? How well do they explain things in layman's language? Do they seem to have your children's best interests at heart? This person will impact your short term and long term life based on how they navigate and achieve the outcome of your case. Can you trust them with your future?

What is the fee structure? Hourly? Retainer? If hourly, do they bill in .25 hour increments? If so, time and expenses accumulate quickly, so make sure you have a mutual understanding of what will be billed for and what won't. This process will involve numerous email exchanges, phone calls and one-on-one meetings as well as meetings with the spouse and his attorney. Know how you will be charged to avoid sticker shock later.

Set up an advisory board of three to five people who can help you through the checks and balances of the process. Ask them to look at agreements and parenting plans so they catch things you or your attorney might not think about. Having multiple eyes, all with one mutual interest, can form an important force to help ensure the best outcome.

Use your attorney for the intended purpose. Remember, your attorney's job isn't your therapist. The legal side of your divorce is business even though at many times it feels very personal. Use your therapist to talk through your emotional and personal plan. Leverage your attorney to help you with the financial and business side of your divorce. Depending on your asset base, you may also need an accountant to discuss financial options and structuring.

In addition to having friends review financial documents, you will need friends with like values to walk through the highs and lows with you – someone you can talk to at 11:32 p.m. Secure two or three friends in your canoe who will be there for you.

You will need to debrief with someone after a visit with an attorney. At times, you will need to confirm that your thinking is on track. Usually these are the friends who have experienced divorce themselves. They may feel called to be there for you, knowing at some point a life crisis of will come knocking on their door, and you will reciprocate.

Taking Flight

On a visit to Wrightsville, NC, I visited the famous Wright Brothers Museum. On one of the walls the three obstacles and subsequent lessons of flight were posted. After much trial and error, the Wright Brothers established three things to be unequivocally overcome and applied in order to take and sustain flight.

These same obstacles and lessons of the Wright brothers are in many ways the same hurdles all the women in this book had to learn in order to ultimately escape their traps. The three obstacles and lessons are:

Obstacle Number One: Lift

In order to take off, you first have to achieve lift. A wing surface has to be designed to take the greatest advantage of the fact that any air particles streaming across the upper and lower surfaces of the wing will keep it aloft.

Within each woman, a resiliency and resolve to change must be established within her core. This resiliency provides the strength and fortitude to not only take the initiative to change, but to use the negative things that want to get in the way of the escape as the very stuff that aids in lifting or providing the initial momentum to keep the process aloft.

Meriam used her contract to evaluate her first and every subsequent move during her release. This allowed the "particles" – the noise from naysayers and her own self-doubt to repel Craig's continued planting of deceit and resistance during the divorce process.

Obstacle Number Two: Power

The Wright Brothers needed a design of a lightweight, high-powered engine along with efficient propellers and a transmission mechanism which would provide enough propulsive force to provide forward motion, lift the heavy machine and sustain that motion while in the air.

Diane used her anger and years of hurt in order to fuel the strength and health she needed to allow herself to press into the wind ahead. This allowed her to convert her anger to power and energy to move her through the flight ahead.

Obstacle Number Three: Control

Stability and direction are required for a successful flight. The air flow over the rapidly turning blades of a propeller-driven plane produces thrust or forward motion. Each blade of the propeller acts as a small rotating force allowing air to flow over its curved surface. It then allows for horizontal "lift" which propels the aircraft forward.

91

The Wright Brothers borrowed this principle of thrust from their knowledge of how a bicycle works. As you start and continue to peddle, momentum ensues.

"Just keep moving forward" was the message all of the women in this book heard and applied. They secured the resources to give them the information needed for the next step as a way to provide momentum. They quickly learned if they stopped at any point along the way, they lost momentary lift, power and control, reducing their go-forward position. Those who delayed, became unsure of the process and pushed the pause button subsequently had to land and go through lift off again each time, delaying their flight and subsequent freedom.

No matter how you are trying to advance in life, momentum is everything in driving the process. As long as you keep going forward in the right direction, your momentum will take you to the desired state. Guaranteed.

BREAKTHROUGH MOMENTS

- List your personal advisory board members on the worksheet on the following page. These are the three to five people you most need in your boat right now.

  Beside each one, write down the one area you need their help with the most during this time. What are the questions or thoughts you need to ask them this week?

Advisor	Help Needed	Questions to Ask
Example: Lori Snow	Childcare	Who may be willing to help or trade?

- What is your number one goal in seeking legal counsel?

- What is your ideal outcome?

- How can you convert the following obstacles into strength and momentum to help you take and keep flight?

  LIFT?

  POWER?

  CONTROL?

BREAK AWAY THOUGHTS

- A change of scenery or a new environment can create the fresh perspective needed to help you create finality and declare your escape. If you can't go to another geographical location, go to a new park for the first time, a private room in a local library or a different section of your house in order to see it from a different angle.

- There is power in numbers. By surrounding yourself with wise counsel, you can feed off their energy and strength as a way to feel positive and resolute about your decision.

- Keep moving! Just as in cycling or flying or anything else that requires ongoing motion, momentum is everything in helping you stay the course. By taking just one step each day, you are one step closer to your freedom.

RESOURCES

http://aviationhistory.info/Wright-Brothers.html

SECTION THREE:
THE FREEDOM

"Wisdom is nothing more than healed pain."

Robert Gary Lee

~CHAPTER SEVEN~

BEWARE OF THE BOOMERANG

Avoiding the Same Trap

Kelli meticulously looked through her closet to find just the right ensemble for the upcoming concert. One of her favorite iconic pop stars from college days was on tour and coming to town. It was important to her to dress up and look the part without appearing as though she was trying too hard. From the closet she pulled the teal blue knit dress that hugged her just right and hung it out so she could start zeroing in on the exact accessories to complement it.

She always enjoyed getting dressed up for Cameron. He seemed to appreciate the way she took care of herself and how she could pull together a striking look on short notice. Cameron was proud to be seen with Kelli, and she loved knowing this. However, Kelli knew in her heart that she wasn't as physically attracted to Cameron as she thought she would be with a future husband who in so many ways seemed ideal. Yet his many other qualities made him a desirable life companion, so she overlooked his shortcomings.

In addition to his continual adoration and love for Kelli, Cameron was financially secure and often expressed to her that everything he owned would be hers. This was comforting in some ways yet as an independent woman, Kelli could never fully leverage it. This wasn't what she wanted in a man – just someone to buy her all the things he wanted her to have.

Somehow, it didn't feel quite right.

The scale frequently tipped from the feeling of generosity to the side of feeling too controlling. Still, Kelli had an unprecedented sense of relief knowing she would never have to worry about money again.

Kelli loved the way Cameron looked at her, the way he was completely devoted and the valiant way in which he had pursued her as his adventure. She often paused to think, *Is this what it's supposed to be like now that I'm finally freed from Mick and 17 years of misery?*

After all this time was she finally at a place of freedom?

Cameron was a man who had no expectations of her achieving a monthly "quota" to contribute to the household, a man who continually expressed his love through her number one love language of touch and a man who gave her more attention that anyone had previously. Had Kelli finally arrived at the lifetime relationship of her dreams?

In spite of all of these positives, occasional friction erupted. Cameron was intense, highly-detailed as well as decisive and uber deliberate in his approach. With a similar level of intensity and drive, Kelli could be much more patient and relaxed in managing the details as well as exercising her level of decisiveness. In everyday communication, Cameron would often ask questions to get to the details of a situation. This had worked well for his career in finance, but often caused a rub in dealing with people who might take the inquisition as unnecessary pressure, focusing on the wrong things in situations that didn't require a micro-perspective.

Kelli felt that pressure.

With the wardrobe choice made earlier, the day before the concert was filled with wedding planning. They were scheduled to visit the wedding and reception venue as well as to meet with the coordinator. Kelli took the afternoon off work which delighted Cameron since he always wanted Kelli to take as much time off as possible. His flexibility as a business owner allowed for ample time off and he often asked Kelli to consider quitting her job or at least cutting back significantly. It was times like this that Cameron's wish seemed appealing, but Kelli loved her work and didn't want to unnecessarily give it up. She decided to stay as malleable as she could to appease Cameron.

While anticipation regarding their future continued to build in Kelli's mind, there was some trepidation. She was often perplexed that she wasn't more outwardly expressive in her joy for the upcoming spring wedding. But she laid her concerns aside when her counselor explained it was probably just the introverted part of her personality not allowing her to externally show more happiness.

While trying on dresses with one of her dearest friends, Kelli wondered if this was supposed to be a kick-your-heels-together-cartwheel experience with girl-like feelings being the most beautiful belle at the ball. Or maybe since this was not her first marriage, she simply wasn't supposed to feel as excited. However, her friend couldn't help but notice and mentioned that Kelli wasn't as happy about the experience as she thought she would be.

It kept occurring to Kelli that she wasn't feeling *anything*. A few times it even felt reminiscent of the numbing out she had in those later years of her marriage when she had to completely desensitize herself to her feelings just to manage the madness.

> *Feeling nothing means we are protecting ourselves from something.*

Was this right? This was supposed to be a joyful time in planning for a lifetime occasion. What more could she possibly want? Cameron frequently reminded her that no one would love her or take care of her the way he did. Kelli believed him – until Cameron's control surfaced in a new and most unbecoming way on the Monday night following the wedding planning. It was so out of character for Cameron – like the blindside attack of Joe Theismann the Monday night he was knocked to the ground with a career-ending blow, his tibia rendered broken and gory in front of millions of fans and viewers.

Over a casual dinner, Cameron and Kelli discussed the financial implication of yet another accident her son had been involved in weeks before. As usual, with the apathy of her ex-husband, Kelli was

The Attractive Trap™ ~ Teresa G. Carey

the one left with the brunt of financial impact for both the positive and negative aspects of their kids' choices. This was just one more area Cameron repeatedly assured Kelli she wouldn't have to worry about. Cameron started drilling into the normal frack of the level of detail regarding the expensive repairs for the other driver's car. Kelli didn't immediately know the facts, so she asked Cameron to allow her to pull up the email on her phone.

One of the quirky things about Kelli was she could remember lines from Honors English Literature in high school, but the recall of numbers didn't come easily. While she searched on her new phone, she couldn't immediately find the email.

Cameron started to grow impatient, asking Kelli, "Where is it? How much is it? Does it cover all costs, including taxes?"

The obsessive questioning sent Kelli over the edge. "Can you wait a freakin' minute, please?" It had been a long, stressful day, and she was doing her best to appease Cameron.

The waiter delivered their sandwiches and salads, exposing him to the pending disagreement. In a cold and degrading tone, Cameron looked at Kelli and said, "Shut the f*&^ up, Kelli. Just shut the f*&^ up."

Like chards of glass piercing through her head and chest, Kelli now felt something. She remembered this feeling. It was akin to how she felt when Mick would call her a name or speak abusively to her. This was much too familiar.

Kelli wondered, who was this man and what did he do with Cameron? In disbelief, she couldn't utter a word. After regaining some semblance of composure, Kelli considered leaving. They had driven her SUV that night and she had the keys in her purse. Not sure what to do, she sat there, knowing her appetite would not return.

It was intriguing to her that Cameron seemed completely unaffected. He enjoyed his meal as though nothing had happened and they were in a state of complete and utter bliss. How could he feign their

100

conflict as non-existent? What did that say about his true emotional sensitivity? Was Kelli open to seeing Cameron's true side for the first time?

Kelli asked Cameron to finish quickly so they could leave. She was unsure where to take this, but she knew he would not be staying at her house that night. Not a word was spoken on the ride home. Kelli asked Cameron to take his suitcase and go stay at a hotel for the night. By that time, it appeared as if Cameron wasn't sure how to handle what he had said, but he wasn't remorseful enough to apologize.

Kelli hardly slept that night and wondered if she should go to the concert with Cameron the next evening. She had anticipated it for months and had never wanted to so desperately attend a concert. But was the concert worth more than her self-respect?

The next morning Cameron showed up early with an apology and a promise that he would never talk to her that way again. Kelli wanted to believe him, but there was a tug inside her that pulled in the direction of knowing this wouldn't be the last time. As she reflected over the past year, there were a few other instances where Cameron had been mildly abusive to her. She reviewed these flashbacks. How had she forgotten them? In spite of her best judgment, Kelly agreed to go to the concert.

Her concern over the lack of wedding excitement expanded into questioning the future of their relationship. Over the next few weeks, Kelli woke up at night with a clear voice in her head telling her to break up with Cameron. She had only heard this voice a few other times and each time it played out as the voice of truth.

But Kelli didn't listen to the voice.

As fate would have it, a tragic event happened in Cameron's life, and his true character was revealed. The validation of what Kelli already knew helped her break the tie with Cameron. It was a gut-wrenching loss yet it became more and more clear to her that what she had started to experience was grooming her for what was to come. In addition to grieving over the lost relationship, Kelli was left once again feeling a deeper loss for what she still couldn't touch. She began to question herself again. Why couldn't she have a healthy relationship?

After all of the work she had done with counselors and personal development, how did she end up here again? That was the question she needed to answer if she planned to stay out of the attractive trap and never return to it.

Emotional and Physical Boomeranging

The average woman leaves a bad relationship seven times before the final break (The National Domestic Violence Hotline, June 10, 2013). Women of faith typically have the longest separations because of the current of pending judgment, fear of divorce and the finality it brings.

Kelli knew this road. She was separated three times from Mick, and after the second separation let Mick move back in only out of convenience, merely as a tenant, because he offered to help pay the mortgage for the house that refused to sell. The agreement never played out and after six more long months of the boomerang, Kelli finally mustered up the courage to make Mick move out for good.

The boomerang with the same man happens for numerous reasons. Many women feel condemnation and constantly ask, "What have I done wrong?"

So in order to right their wrong, they go back, hoping to find the answer to their faults. In fact, the feelings of self-guilt can be so strong that 65% of women with lifelong relationships with the church end up leaving because they no longer feel comfortable with themselves. Unsure of who they are, at a minimum they are certain they no longer fit in with what should be the most welcoming solace. Most feel they are judged and put into a rare box and may even slide themselves into victimization. Few places exist where they feel as if they truly belong.

What is Wrong Can Seem So Right

Many of the aspects of Kelli's and Cameron's relationship seemed so right on the surface. Yet in reality, these very signs indicated the relationship was actually unhealthy.

In addition to other signs, you may want to look out for these:

The Promise of Financial Security

While the financial security seemed appealing, just as it was used as a ploy to attract Kelli to the relationship, it was also used to keep her in the relationship. The offer to take care of her, insinuating that everything he had was hers and always offering to pay for her necessities were several ways Cameron tried to insert his sense of control. What was guised as protection and security was actually demonstrated as control.

Cameron played off the void her ex-husband left in the financial arena. Kelli's ex-husband was financially irresponsible and unemployed a few times. Kelli was frequently left to figure out the financial puzzle. Now to have some sort of financial promise seemed freeing. Yet it was truly restricting her from making the choices she needed to make in order to honor herself.

> *"Over-the-top" behaviors usually are attributed to an over compensation for something else in that person or in the relationship that is missing.*

Grandiosity

After dating for just one month, Cameron invited Kelli on a trip. Just a few weeks later, he gave her a credit card. Even though Kelli refused to use it, just accepting it allowed Cameron to lay an unentitled claim on her. He was always offering to buy Kelli clothes and their first Christmas together was over the top with expensive jewelry and electronics.

Kelli wasn't quite sure what to make of it. No one had ever treated her with such generosity yet in many ways it raised suspicions in her mind regarding Cameron's motives.

While one friend told her, "Give his gifts back and send him packing," others claimed what seemed lavish to her was just normal behavior to him, given his financial status.

Which was it? Kelli wasn't sure. She just knew that he seemed crazy about her and it fed her feeling of worthiness.

Over time, Kelli knew she was the only one who could live out her own self-worth. She also remembered that early on she had confessed to Cameron how gifts had been a rarity with her ex-husband. Yet another gap Cameron plotted to fill.

The Captivated Complex

Feeling so loved and adored sent a rush to Kelli's heart. Dressing up and being told she was beautiful satisfied her little girl longing of wanting to feel like a princess. While she heard about women being treated as "arm candy," she was sure this wasn't the same. She was a strong and smart business woman. She knew Cameron appreciated her intellect and sense of humor. However, she also knew he all but worshiped her appearance and what he thought she represented physically, and he wasn't afraid to let her know.

How much was too much? When he was sitting in the chair of the living room and asked her to turn around for him while he stared and admired her, was that over the top? When he insisted they sit side by side regardless of the restaurant table arrangement was that out of alignment with normal?

Cameron had picked up on Kelli's feeling unloved and unappreciated in her first marriage. He knew the desire of her heart was to feel worthy and valued. So this became like a fix for both of them. Cameron filled his tank of worth by being seen with a pretty girl. Kelli felt beautiful because of Cameron's doting. It seemed to work for both of them.

Avoid Being Attracted to the Wrong Relationships

We are drawn to and attract what is familiar and comfortable. Kelli's therapist often quipped, "Kelli, the devil you know is always preferable to the one you don't."

Regardless of how crazy certain people in our lives may be, we learn better than anyone else how to live with them and we become skilled in how to handle them. Predictability starts to unfold and before we know it we become the expert in knowing how to deal with this attractive, albeit abusive, behavior. That approach results in a strange yet settling comfort.

Often, we are attracted to others who help fill a need within us. If we are withdrawn, the happy, narcissistic charmer may swing our mood the other way, but only until he drops us on our heads. If we are sad or depressed, those with drama may put new interest in our lives, turning it into an unpredictable ride.

The net result in any relationship when we are looking either consciously or subconsciously to fill a need within ourselves, is dysfunction and discord. If this becomes psychologically fulfilling and stimulating, it can escalate into dependency.

In every boomerang relationship, a deficiency of self-worth plays a major role. Not valuing our worth is one of the biggest factors in attracting, staying in and returning back to a flawed relationship. It seems easier to pay the price of unhappiness versus the price of loneliness.

Deborah Ward, relationship expert and author of "Sense and Sensitivity," refers to the problem as the "familiarity principle." She shows how people she terms as highly sensitive, or HSPs face bigger and more unique challenges in finding and maintaining healthy relationships. Ward says HSPs feel and demonstrate intimacy and empathy at deep levels and often don't get it reciprocated. They are most likely to attract narcissists "who sense our empathy, compassion and our need for intimacy and use it to fuel their own desires." Most women who attract abusive men are highly sensitive and the trapper intuitively senses, knows and plays it to his advantage.

Ward states that "studies have shown that we are all attracted to what is familiar to us, and that repeated exposure to certain people will increase our attraction toward them. This is a subconscious process that we're not even aware of or have any awareness of making such a choice. We are attracted to familiar people because we consider them to be safe and unlikely to cause harm. This doesn't just apply to people we've actually seen before or to people who look familiar, but also to people who behave in ways that are familiar to us."

A classic example is when women marry men like their fathers, even bad fathers who were abusive or alcoholics. If this is the case, we will be most likely attracted to men who are abusive or alcoholics, not because we find them attractive but because we find their behavior so familiar. When bad is all you've ever known, it's still familiar. This is the primary reason why people find it so difficult to leave and stay out of hurtful relationships. It's a subconscious reaction.

Ward encourages us to become aware of the patterns in our relationships. We can only control what we know about. Through this new level of awareness, we can create a new pattern. Striving for awareness and responding to our new knowledge will break the cycle of blaming ourselves or replaying the tape that "we only like the bad guys" or "I always end up with this kind of person."

Ask yourself, "Who taught me this?" With complete introspection, we soon discover that our moms and/or dads conditioned us for certain types of relationships. The point isn't to blame our parents or to victimize ourselves. It is to proactively choose who we want in our lives so that we start to attract a new type of person.

Many say it takes at least one year for every four to five years of marriage to break the cycle and start over. This may not be a hard and fast rule. But it takes much patience, grace and practice in addition to a heightened awareness of what behaviors we use to attract certain people into our lives. This is the only way to keep ourselves from returning to the comfortable trap we worked so diligently to escape from.

BREAKTHROUGH MOMENTS

- In what ways are you being controlled today or have you been controlled in the past?

- What does it feel like?

- In addition to writing a list of the characteristics you want in a future mate, write down how you will feel when you are with him.

  Characteristics:

  How I Will Feel:

- Why is knowing how something should feel more significant than what you list as characteristics of a behavior or a person?

- How does this reinforce the power of your intuition, your truth and Spirit?

BREAK AWAY THOUGHTS

- Control can be overt (blatantly abusive and restrictive verbally and physically) as well as covert (money, guarantees or promises of the best, over the top with nonstop lavish praise and affection).

- Pay attention if you are in a situation or relationship that doesn't give you peace and doesn't allow you to maintain your power. What about it is diminishing for you?

- If the place you find yourself seems eerily familiar in any way, it's probably because you've been there before. Make sure it's a place you want to revisit. Get in touch with how the trap feels so you sense it when you are getting close to a trap again.

RESOURCES

"The Five Love Languages" by Gary D. Chapman, Reprint, 2015

Psychology Today, July 10, 2013; Deborah Ward, "The Familiarity Principle of Attraction"

Why We Repeatedly Choose the Wrong Relationships by Jeannie Assimos, Vice President, Content, E-Harmony

"Dating Do's and Don'ts" by Julia Flood, YourTango.com

~CHAPTER EIGHT~

RESTORATION

Discovering Hope

On a crisp fall Sunday morning, Sara found her way into the church and discreetly sat in a pew with three vacant seats. Down the row and all around her there were couples. Was there even a place for her to belong? Most every Sunday when Sara found her way to church, she also found sadness. She invariably felt loneliness scream from the empty seats beside her. However, on this particular Sunday, she discovered hope.

After the service, as everyone was mingling, a woman sitting down the row from Sara approached her. She knowingly looked into Sara's eyes and said, "I know how you feel. I was single for many years before I met my husband." She then captured Sara's purest emotion by vulnerably relating to her, "You seem so sad, and I understand."

Tears streamed down Sara's face and her newfound friend, Janette, asked if she could give her a hug. They sat down and Janette briefly shared how her story of divorce, singleness and loneliness turned into one of hope, faithfulness and completion. Sara began to feel like someone at church really understood. She realized others might be sitting within a short circumference who may also have a similar story, but would never share it.

In that moment, Sara felt a freedom that was hard to explain. For her, having someone validate her singleness within the church was crucial. Her deep faith and upbringing was an ally to her. Yet at times, it also posed as the enemy in preventing her from living authentically with this unfamiliarity of marital breakdown. Knowing someone else acknowledged her, she wasn't invisible in the pew, and the road she had chosen was understood and affirmed positively by another Christian was indeed powerful.

The irony was sobering to Sara. Something else happened within her that day she hadn't expected. She no longer needed validation from others who would never understand her decision to fully live out who God intended her to be. From that moment on, Sara didn't allow another person or circumstance to define how she viewed her purpose or her plan for her life. In some strange way, she knew this was God's plan all along.

Sara saw beauty rising from ashes. She knew the promises she had made regarding her hopeful future and her trust in God set her free. She was stronger than ever.

She vowed to move forward with no regrets, full of purpose and intentionality to claim who she was. Seeking others' approval had robbed her of her ability to move forward and had kept her captive far longer than it should have. Sara knew she served the One who came to set the captive free.

Shame, guilt, and the perception of ridicule had held her back. She now realized it was dishonoring to her Creator to allow others to define her worth. She was ready to chart her course ahead with boldness and courage.

She never again entered church through the "same door" or sat in the "same seat" with the same thoughts about herself. Sara knew she was continuing to become a whole woman.

Claiming Your Purpose and Passion

In the book, "Man's Search for Meaning," Victor Frankl highlights the one thing all survivors of the Holocaust had in common. When each survivor was interviewed after their horrific hell, they all shared one key attribute – they kept their eyes on their future purpose, knowing they had something yet to do in life. Each one was determined their time couldn't be cut short or end needlessly in the concentration camps. With the grit of frail survival, they knew dying would mean they wouldn't get to accomplish what they felt was their life mission.

Remember the vision, mission and values you worked on while in the trap? Remember how they kept you going? These values were recommended to remind you of your purpose and worth. If you tucked them away, now is the time to dust them off. Go back and reread Chapter Five – Envision and Plan Your Strategy.

Now that you are fully free, it is time to live out your vision! What is that vision? How does it connect to your mission or purpose and what do you have yet to accomplish in life?

If you knew you could do anything you wanted and not fail, what would you do?

In a perfect world, you would be able to combine your greater mission in life with your passion. To integrate both of these allows you to have a deeper spiritual meaning for work so that it's not just work, but rather your calling or purpose.

Your calling is defined as what only you were created to do. For example, my business is built on coaching leaders in the workplace to optimize their full leadership potential. It's a strategic part of my bigger calling. I'm fortunate that I get to tie both of these together. And I don't believe it's an accident.

As a fifth grader, I was asked by my teacher to write one statement about what I wanted to do in my future. Several years ago, while going through keepsakes during my parents' move from the house where I grew up, I happened to stumble upon my response. It was articulated in a way that an 11 year-old would best claim. The three-hole punched, tattered paper was the canvas for the answer. It simply read, "I want to teach others to help them be the best they can be."

Recently, I refined my purpose and calling with two words: liberating greatness (Source: WomenDoingWell.org). Every day, I have the opportunity to liberate greatness within the leaders I coach, my children and my husband. The way I facilitate and embrace our time together can either liberate or restrict. It can unleash harm, limit potential, or it can optimize and liberate greatness.

I believe you are great. My heart was called to write this book because I know there are women like you who need to be liberated so they can actualize their worth and ultimately their wholeness.

After my divorce, I took the time to step back and ask one of the most powerful questions any of us can ever ask ourselves, "What has everything I've done up to this point in my life prepared me to do?"

Here is the advice I gave to myself as well as the steps involved, and I challenge you to do the same:

1- Make a list of all the roles, jobs or careers you've had. What did you like most about each one? One of the roles I accepted was Chairperson of the Teacher Appreciation Committee at my children's school. It was fulfilling to work with a team in celebrating the great work the school staff accomplished in serving our children. An earlier job in my career was Senior Trainer for a document technology company. I thrived in knowing I was delivering and facilitating learning for others who would leverage the information to improve their sales and ultimately grow revenue for their team and the entire organization.

2- For each role you've listed, what strengths did you leverage? Are you a good planner, organizer or an action-oriented executor? Be sure to list your passions and strengths in the BREAKTHROUGH MOMENTS Section at the end of this chapter. For example, some of my key strengths are creativity, curiosity and communication. I've used these strengths both in volunteer roles as well as work positions.

What strengths did you list for yourself? When you and those who know you best look at this list of strengths, how do they come together to help point you toward your greater purpose?

Perhaps you cannot do today what you want to do. Maybe you need more education, training or work experience. Do you want to work in a completely different field? What will it take? Who can you enlist as a mentor?

Do you want to start your own business but you don't yet have the money or runway to get the revenue built to support yourself? Work for a competitor first. Ask other entrepreneurs to help you refine your idea and concept so you can write a business plan. Many free resources exist to coach and guide you (listed in the Resources section).

One of my friends, Annette, was divorced six years ago. Some of her friends connected her to a pre-school teaching position at a local church as a way to invest her talent and make some income. Annette openly admits she makes little money, yet the people at the preschool have been her rock in supporting and sustaining her through some of the most difficult times over the past several years.

What this job and the team she works with means to Annette was summed up when she recently attended the funeral of someone whose brother's life was taken much too soon. When she saw the group of friends surround, support and love on their friend and her family, it caused her to pause.

She asked herself, "Who would love and encourage me if this happened to me?" She knew it probably wasn't a long-time group of friends, but rather her newest co-workers and friends who had embraced and loved her since her divorce, the ones who held her up, even at her lowest point.

About a year ago, Annette was asked by a friend to help start a business working part-time, using her college education in journalism and broadcasting to help build the communication and marketing strategy for the business. Today, she is leveraging her education and enjoying building something with a friend, in addition to continuing her part-time job at the preschool.

Annette also speaks about her newfound outlet and fondness for art and painting. What has long been a hobby is unfolding as a true talent with many of her friends now boldly challenging her to start selling some of the pieces she has created.

With all this happening in her life, Annette has definitely found purpose – at least for this season. She openly admits this may not be what she does forever and it may not be "the" thing, but Annette knows and trusts she's doing what she's called to do right now. Each of her interests and experiences have been serendipitously woven together for such a time as this. So she is pressing in, and listening carefully as the path leads to the next step, or possibly a different path.

While none of us may begin where we ultimately end up, the important thing is that we start to slowly move toward identifying, embracing and over time – trusting that we will realize our mission, passion and purpose. The expectation in this chapter isn't that you will find all three within these pages (however, you *just might* have that revelation – if you're ready for it!). At a minimum, you can empower yourself to start the process.

In a recent issue of "Psychology Today" (March 15, 2015), Guy Winch, Ph.D., licensed psychologist, keynote speaker and author, coins the "7 Habits of Truly Genuine People." One of those seven key habits is, "Genuine people forge their own paths."

Winch goes on to state, "Being authentic is not just about what you think or say but what you *do* and how you are in the world. Being guided by an internal compass means not having to follow the conventional or typical routes others take to achieve their goals. Therefore, genuine people search for and discover their own unique way of pursuing their passions and purpose, often forging an entirely new path as they do."

Answer this question honestly: "If time and money didn't matter, what would I do?"

Allow yourself to feel the freedom in answering this question. Maybe you can't do "it" today, but what can you do — starting now — to move in that direction?

Accepting, Loving and Caring For Yourself

Now that you are starting to work on your restoration and reclaim your passion, it is important to continue to recognize your significance and how you were created by special design.

Before we can love another we have to love ourselves. We can learn how our beautiful broken mess is being pulled back together into a mosaic that is much more becoming than what we thought was possible.

In his popular work, "The Five Love Languages," Gary Chapman unveils five universal ways we express and take in love. These include: touch, words of affirmation, quality time, acts of service and gifts. We all tend to have a preference for one or two of these in how we relate to others.

My primary love language is touch. During the rocky years of marriage, healthy and wanted touch was scarce. After I filed for divorce, I knew I would want and seek out touch as a primary part of any future relationship. In the meantime, during the separation and before I was ready to love again, I deeply wanted touch to be expressed in healthy ways.

It occurred to me that I could receive massages, which would be healthy physically, emotionally and mentally. I was concerned that I could not possibly fit massages into my new budget. Fortunately, several low cost quality massage franchises were emerging in the market around that time, so I was able to arrange the budget perfectly to satisfy my need for touch.

If you are wondering how to best take care of yourself, think about how the answers to these questions can help you show the much needed attention and love you so richly deserve:

- How have I taken care of others in a way that expressed my love? Take care of yourself that same way. Any of us would buy a massage for a loved one for whom we wanted to show affection, if circumstances allowed for it.

This may be the first time you have the real option to take care of yourself. It's long overdue.

- What would you do for yourself if you were a child again? We can all embrace loving the innocent inner child that exists within us in a nurturing and meaningful way.

- What boundaries do I need to set to protect myself and invest in me right now? Plenty of time exists to invest in others. Now is the time to reconfigure your life and this will take time and energy. It is not selfish to block off the time you need to invest what is needed to rebuild and reclaim your life.

Our bodies, minds and emotions have just been through the equivalent of a marathon with the endurance of marital discord and the process of divorce. The additional stamina needed to make it through to this part of the journey can set the stage for a myriad of health issues. Sleep, physical and emotional challenges are par for the course during and after divorce.

At the University of Utah, Dr. Nancy Henry, medical researcher, found that marital dysfunction can increase our risk of heart disease by 20 percent. Interestingly, the researchers stated in the reported data, "It's clear that the association of stress and heart health is stronger in women." In addition to the potential of heart problems (and the certainty of a broken heart), they found a myriad of other presenting health issues that can surface in divorce.

Because the body has been living under more than normal stress, the adrenal gland can over-function, inviting numerous metabolic disorders such as diabetes, high blood pressure and weight gain.

Henry states, "From research we know women tend to base their self-concept on relationships, how they are doing, how things are going for them. And we think that's the reason we've shown that negative relationship issues seem to take a greater toll on women emotionally and physically."

Tim Smith, PhD, a professor of psychology at the University of Utah, stated as part of the same research, "Although bad marriages can contribute to depression in men, the physiological problems seem to show up only in women."

The National Institute of Mental Health explains that a major life event, such as divorce, can lead to increased stress and risk for depression. Plus, women are more susceptible to mood disorders "due to hormonal factors that can influence the brain chemicals that regulate mood."

So now we have even more compelling reasons to love and care for ourselves. If we break down, it will be impossible to do those things we have yet to do in life and to love others.

The following simple steps list the necessary recovery and personal energy for moving forward:

1- Get the needed rest. Make sure at least seven to eight hours of sleep per night are par for the course. Those who get sufficient sleep live longer, report improved memory, curb anxiety and depression and improve overall physical and mental performance (health.com).

2- Let go of every "nice-to-do" thing in your life. Re-evaluate the "need-to-dos." If someone else can do it, let it go. Give yourself grace to abandon certain things, at least for this season. If you still feel as passionately about the cause in two years, and you have the bandwidth, jump back in.

3- Divorce others who aren't supporting and nourishing you. You only have so much time and energy. This is not the time to placate "energy vampires." The energy you do have should go into restoring your life. Engage in the circles and with people who only show you unconditional love and support. This may mean leaving long-time relationships, social groups or even your church.

4- Journal and continue to replace your old tapes and stories with new ones about who are, how you will live your worth and all of the goodness that will come into your life.

5- Positively affirm yourself multiple times daily. One of my friends was told to tell herself something positive at pre-determined times each day (at each meal, at bathroom times…you get the picture). Another friend frequently writes messages to herself on her bathroom mirror with a marker, proclaiming encouraging phrases and verses that keep her focused on moving forward. Recently, she wrote, "I will not be denied," on the middle of her mirror, to remind herself she will never again be denied the opportunity to create the life she wants and deserves to live.

Paying It Forward

"It's really none of your business," the man sternly stated with his eyes of steel laced with anger.

Like hell it isn't, thought Rachel. Watch me make it my business.

While seated for dinner with her new husband, she could hardly believe what unfolded. At the table just a few yards away, a one-sided argument had erupted. A restaurant guest who may have had one too many, or who had just simply missed the lesson on how to treat another human being, had begun to threaten and call his date lewd names. His hand landed intentionally and hurtfully on her sunburned thigh and contact finished with a tight squeeze as other guests at nearby tables had now become onlookers. With this type of behavior too eerily reminiscent in her former relationship, Rachel jumped at the sound of the leg slap, ready to move into confront mode.

As Rachel moved in the direction of the scene, the man sent money with the waitress to pay their check. Not yet seeing Rachel and still embroiled in his fit of anger, words of venom secreted from his mouth. Rachel knew if the couple left before she intervened it could be night of verbal, mental and perhaps even physical abuse for the woman she didn't really know – yet somehow strangely felt akin to on a spiritual level. In many ways, this was her opportunity to help herself and all of the women who were trapped.

As the woman started to cry, Rachel's legs reflexed unconsciously and uncontrollably. Her body moved in response to her heart. She didn't have a choice about her reaction.

Rachel calmly told the man he was out of control. In anger he stormed from the table to leave the restaurant. As even more tears fell from the woman's eyes, she shared with Rachel that her much older boyfriend had been too zealous that afternoon, drinking on their vacation. When he drank, she confided, he always resorted to abuse.

Rachel pleaded with the young woman not to go back to the hotel where the man might return to continue his lashing out and to hurt her even more. The young woman explained that her boyfriend had the airline tickets in the room and she would have to work fast to catch a cab to beat him back to the hotel. Another guest came to the table to help Rachel coach the young woman on her next steps.
While the women were talking, Rachel's mind reeled back to what was supposed to be a date night out with her former husband, Syd.

She thought about how he tormented her throughout the dinner for forgetting her ring. Then he started to grow angrier as Rachel told him her honest feelings about a business he was considering buying. When he asked for her input on his decision, she gently told Syd it was a risk they couldn't afford as bills had begun to stack up from his months of unemployment. Syd grew furious, accusing Rachel of never supporting him, while she was the one balancing the four kids and work to keep the family afloat.

The anger escalated then evolved into silence, Syd's greatest weapon of aggression. They sat through the rest of the dinner with Syd saying nothing yet looking at her in disdain. Meanwhile it had become obvious to the waitress and the nearby tables that trouble was in full force at the coveted window side table.

Rachel choked back the tears as they sat in silence, all the while trying sporadically to engage Syd in light-hearted conversation. He refused to engage, accelerating the painful embarrassment and obvious derailment of the evening.

The final blow came for Rachel when Syd told her to get out her credit card. "You've managed to ruin this dinner so by God you'll pay for it."

To put a final stake in the night, Rachel did as she was told and took out the credit card. She knew this was another guidepost for her that she must escape. Syd was indeed the person she knew he was, and this was just more evidence of his true character.

On the erratic speed-breaking ride home that evening, Rachel knew she was at a point where she had to stop giving Syd any more of her heart or mind. Even her requested thoughts weren't safe with Syd and he had proven yet again he couldn't be trusted with any part of her.

As her familiar tears moistened the pillow that night, Rachel promised herself she would never again allow Syd to embarrass her publicly. She would find a way of escape, no matter what.

As Syd's unpredictable behavior became more frequent and rapid fire, the moment for Rachel to keep her promise to herself showed up sooner than expected. Just weeks later at a restaurant near their home, Syd's public crazy factor again surfaced.

Rachel recommended the new local neighborhood spot after having delectable appetizers and wine there with a friend the first week it opened. She had heard equally good reviews on the entrees and recommended it to Syd as a possibility for date night. Syd went for this nearby option since they were leaving teenage kids home alone for just a couple of hours.

After being seated and looking at the nightly offerings, Syd flung his menu across the table. "This looks disgusting," he claimed, quickly casting blame on Rachel for the choice.

Knowing there were many options on the menu she knew Syd had eaten at other places and typically enjoyed, she was shocked.

"Do you want to leave?" she quickly offered.

"Of course not," Syd retorted. "Where else are we going to go at this late time and still make it back in time for the kids? I can't believe you recommended this place!" Driving the dagger deeper, he followed with a giant exhale and the rolling of his eyes.

At that moment, something within Rachel snapped. Strength and empowerment rose within her. She knew what she must do.

Looking Syd squarely in the eyes, Rachel retorted, "You'll have to eat alone if you stay here. I've been treated disrespectfully at a restaurant for the last time. I'm walking home."

Rachel "got her groove back," and in that moment she took her power back from Syd. Increasingly, he seemed to be taking his abuse to public places where he thought Rachel wouldn't be able to keep her footing. It was a logical form of control. The more Rachel reflected on it in later months during the divorce, she saw it as the trap it was. Syd wanted to see if she would take the bait. He would bait her by losing it in public, and then point the finger of blame at her.

This time, Rachel didn't take the bait. She took control of her situation and did what any self-respecting woman would do. She got up, walked out and left Syd in shock at the restaurant table.

As she started the trek home in high heels and a skirt and silk shirt in the 80 plus degree heat, the thought occurred to her that she wasn't alone. She could call in reinforcements. As she approached the neighborhood drug store, she realized she could outsmart this unfortunate situation even more. She went into the store and called her neighbor to see if she could come to the store to pick her up. Rachel was unable with the time and circumstances allowed to explain the details of what had unfolded. Hearing her need, the neighbor agreed to come immediately.

This was the first time Rachel had asked for help, and it multiplied her confidence to know she had not only escaped her dinner cell but also had been mentally sharp enough to enlist a partner in her escape.

Rachel knew Syd would feel shamed even though she had calmly and quickly left the scene of his familiar crime. She also knew he would leave and start to look for her. She could see him through the store window and could only hope he didn't see her. She wanted him to realize what he had done. And even more importantly, Rachel was finished taking his emotional abuse at restaurants or anywhere else.
As predicted, Syd crept by slowly in the car, knowing this would be a logical respite for a runaway wife while making it home on a smoldering and humid evening. Rachel managed to duck out of the way, but not fast enough. Syd saw a fleeting portion of her profile.

But Rachel knew he wouldn't come after her. At this point he was guessing what Rachel might say or do and the potential of not having control of her would be beyond what he could handle.

In a matter of minutes, her ride arrived and Rachel told her neighbor exactly what Syd had done. The disclosure helped drive a stake in the ground. Speaking the truth liberated her to boldness and made empowerment feel easier than ever before.

As Rachel's mind returned to the event of the present evening, the waitress and manager leapt to the rescue to provide cab fare while enlisting the help of another staff member to watch the exited man's next move. It was evident the man was headed down the beach in the opposite direction.

Rachel begged the young woman to get her ticket and head to the airport. The young woman made the promise as she quickly and discreetly left in a cab for her hotel.

As Rachel returned to her seat next to her new loving and respectful husband, a few tears of her own flowed down her cheeks. Had she been wrong to get involved? No! What if someone had done this for her, she wondered.

As Rachel finally pushed "STOP" on the reruns in her mind as well as this evening's episode, she knew she was destined for a time such as this. This was a small part of what she was prepared to do. She was now purposed and emboldened to bring other women to rescue — if even in a small way — at a restaurant.

BREAKTHROUGH MOMENTS

- What approval are you still seeking that you need to let go of so you can truly move forward?

- What is the one thing you "can't not do" in your life? What do you need to do to claim it?

- Who are your energy givers? How can you share more time with them?

- Who are your energy takers or vampires? What can you do to distance yourself from them?

- What one step can you take starting today to keep your recovery going and your energy strong?

- What are three to five areas in which you have both strength and passion?

- What research can you start working on to help you clarify the interests you should begin to pursue? Talking with others? Online research?

BREAK AWAY THOUGHTS

- You don't need to have your ultimate purpose in life figured out now. Claim it, write it down, and it will continue to unfold each day.

- You are not alone in figuring out how your uniqueness of strengths and passions come together in providing options for how you best use your talents. Tap into them.

- Obey the law of "cognitive resonance" – only be around those who make deposits into your soul instead of withdrawals.

RESOURCES

www.womendoingwell.org

"Bad Marriages Take Health Toll on Women: Study Shows Marital Discord Hurts Women's Physical Health More Than Men's," by Bill Hendrick, reviewed by Louise Chang, MD.: webmd.com/heart-disease/news/20090304/bad-marriages-take-health-toll-on-women?page=2, March 4, 2009

http://www.health.com/health/gallery/0,,20459221_4,00.html

Association of Career Professionals – www.acpinternational.org

FastTrac and The Kauffman Foundation business planning programs –www.fasttrac.org

Small Business Administration – www.sba.gov

~CHAPTER NINE~

FINDING THE TREASURE

Leaving the Remnants Behind

Sherry was consumed by tears as she hit the rapid stride toward her wedding. All the joy, peace and contentment she had come to know these past 18 months seemed to take a back seat to the overbearing sadness within her – now apparent on her face. The celebration of her pending nuptials seemed remotely distant, even though just hours within her reach.

She stretched out her foot on the path to meet the promise of light ahead. Extending as far as possible, Sherry was almost to the shadow of the beam closest to her. She looked over her shoulder. She needed just a glimpse of what had started to hold her back. Her view revealed a slight tear in her coat and a small amount of fabric stuck to the rose bush just a few inches behind her.

Laboring for what seemed like hours to free herself from the thorny nest, Sherry was intent on avoiding additional damage to her garment. As she worked meticulously to release the slight amount of fabric from the bush without pricking her fingers on the painful tips of the thorny stems, she had a new thought rush through her mind – she could simply take off the coat and leave it behind.

Sherry had worn this coat out of convenience. Admittedly it also carried a familiar hint of nostalgia. It wasn't the warmest, prettiest or most functional coat she owned, but it had been part of her wardrobe for more years than she cared to remember.

Her mother gave it to her, and it kept resurfacing as a comfortable and timeless piece. Leaving it behind would seem like abandoning a familiar acquaintance. But the more she considered the option, the freer she felt. She remembered how she would look at herself in the coat and notice it really didn't flatter her best style or play to her best features. One friend even candidly shared that it looked a little frumpy. Most of the time, it overshadowed her sleek and envious figure.

Most importantly, it camouflaged the potential of who she really was underneath the layer of faux wool blend.

Could she part with it? How would she feel throughout this season as she reached for the coat in her closet, only to remember her conscious and willing decision to leave it behind? How much regret might she feel, knowing she gave up something that had been a part of her family for so many years?

> *Giving up what once may have seemed priceless is often the only way to be completely free.*

With a certainty she had felt few times in life, Sherry was finally ready to give up what had originally seemed a precious heirloom. It was the only way to be completely freed from the rosebush that had seemed so attractive.

Ahead of her, she could feel the sunshine. The path was filled with brightness and warmth. She didn't need a coat to cover who she was. What had seemed like a gift, now seemed like an unnecessary burden she had kept out of obligation. The real gift was in finally letting go. She no longer had to wear something that was uncomfortable – something that hid who she truly was and could be.

It was final. Sherry took off the coat and left it behind. Never looking back, she wasn't tempted to return to pick the remaining coat threads from the thorn. To do so would only delay what lay ahead.

A future she had been promised would be filled with rare and beautiful treasures far beyond what she could even hope or imagine.

Recognizing the Treasure

In her book, "One Thousand Gifts," author Ann Voskamp tells her story as a farmwife in rural Canada. Not a place she claims she would have chosen to raise a family or how she would have elected to blossom and use her writing talents. Because of her love for her devoted husband and his commitment to his call of farming, she chose to embrace the agricultural life. While many would proclaim the often brutal winters and rugged agrarian lifestyle a huge sacrifice, Ann celebrates it as an opportunity to love the simple, be in the present and give thanks for everyday blessings.

In the midst of what many would lament as discontent, she decides to daily list the everyday "gifts" she receives in return for the investment she is making in her marriage and family. In her best-selling book, Ann chooses to focus on the upside take away of her circumstances, reminding us of the power of optimism and glass half-full thinking.

On a recent Google search of the term, "How to Search for Treasure" there were more than 87,700,000 responses to this coveted secret. Contained in this search was Wikihow's all-knowing answer:

"Treasure hunting can take place in exotic locations, at the flea market, in your town or even in your backyard. Knowing how to find treasure, though, depends on what type of adventure you are seeking and how far you are willing to go to find it."

Can we really take something that was so excruciatingly painful, so incredibly harmful and so disruptive to "normalcy" and look for the treasure in it? Increasingly, research suggests we can and should.

In the March 22, 2012, issue of NY Times magazine, Jim Rendon wrote about "Post-Traumatic Stress's Surprisingly Positive Flip Side." The article chronicles the story of a wounded soldier in the Iraqi war, Beltran, who lost his short term memory due to injury and trauma. At the time of the article, Rendon described Beltron's new term for

PTSD (Post Traumatic Stress Disorder) as *Post Traumatic Stress Development.*

Rendon goes on to state, "People growing in positive ways from hardship is so embedded in our culture that few researchers even noticed it was there to be studied," especially when correlated to PTSD. He shares a story about Richard Tedeschi, a psychologist at the University of North Carolina, Charlotte, who is both a researcher and a clinician, and discovered this in a roundabout way while looking for a new research project.

Tedeschi stated, "Who do I want to know the most about, distressed or violent or crazy people? Instead, I think I want to know about wise people. Perhaps I'll learn something myself."

Rendon writes that Tedeschi and Lawrence Calhoun, who is also a psychologist at U.N.C., started their research by interviewing survivors of severe injuries. He then went on to survey older people who had lost their spouses. Person after person told them the same thing: "They wished deeply they had not lost a spouse or been paralyzed, but nonetheless, the experience changed them for the better."

"Patterns began to emerge in a follow-up study of more than 600 trauma survivors," Rendon wrote. According to the study, people reported positive change in five areas:

1- they had a renewed appreciation for life
2- they found new possibilities for themselves
3- they felt more personal strength
4- their relationships improved
5- they felt spiritually more satisfied

Tedeschi developed an inventory to track and measure the phenomenon, and in 1995, he and Calhoun coined the term "Post-traumatic growth." "Experiencing growth in the wake of trauma,

Tedeschi asserts, is far more common than PTSD and can even coexist with it."

Post-Traumatic Stress Development... beauty from ashes, lemonade from lemons and treasure from trash. That's what an optimistic outlook, upon freedom from the trap, can unleash.

I'm thrilled to declare that all the women with the sad and pain-rendering life experiences described in this book absolutely have this perspective.

They all currently report the blessings of "being on the other side" of the pain and stress from an irreparable relationship with a man who tried to take away who they were through repeated mental, emotional, spiritual and/or physical abuse.

> *The most horrific or even the mildest trauma can produce some of the most meaningful and priceless treasures.*

The good news is that not every woman trapped in an abusive relationship suffers from PTSD. However, the PTSD website of the United States Department of Veteran Affairs reports: "Trauma is most common in women – with five out of ten women experiencing some type of traumatic event. Women tend to experience different traumas than men. While both men and women report many of the same symptoms of PTSD – hyperarousal, re-experiencing, avoidance, and numbing – some symptoms are more common for women than for men."

The website goes on to say that women are more than twice as likely to develop PTSD than men (10% for women and 4% for men). A few reasons for this difference might be:

- Women are more likely to experience some type of assault.

- Sexual assault is more likely to cause PTSD than many other events.
- Women may be more likely to blame themselves for traumatic experiences than men.

What should a woman do with herself, as a way of working through all this suffering on the other side? Learning the lessons and applying them seems to be a great start.

Dr. Henry Cloud, mentioned earlier in reference to his best-selling Boundaries book with Dr. John Townsend, has written another bestselling work that all of us who have endured hardship should read: "Never Go Back: the 10 Things You Will Never Do Again."

Cloud describes how we can have "awakenings" and once we have these, we can't and won't ever go back to the way things were before.

In the July 24, 2014, issue of *Success Magazine*, these 10 areas are summed up as the "10 Things Successful People Won't Ever Do Again." Cloud calls them the "10 doorways of learning we go through to never return again."

1- **Return to what hasn't worked.** Whether a job, or a broken relationship that was ended for a good reason, we should never go back to the same thing, expecting different results, without something being different.

2- **Do anything that requires them to be someone they are not.** In everything we do, we have to ask ourselves, "Why am I doing this? Am I suited for it? Does it fit me? Is it sustainable?" If the answer is 'No' to any of these questions, you need a very good reason to proceed.

3- **Try to change another person.** When you realize you cannot force someone into doing something, you give others freedom and allow them to experience the consequences. In doing so, you find your own freedom as well.

4- **Believe they can please everyone.** Once you understand it truly is impossible to please everyone, you begin to live purposefully, seeking to please the right people.

5- **Choose short-term comfort over long-term benefit.** Once successful people know they want something that requires a painful, time-limited step, they do not mind the painful step because it gets them to a long-term benefit. Living out this principle is one of the most fundamental differences between successful and unsuccessful people, both personally and professionally.

6- **Trust someone or something that appears flawless.** It is natural for us to be drawn to things and people that appear "incredible." We love excellence and should always be looking for it. We should pursue people who are great at what they do, employees who are high-performers, dates who are exceptional people, friends who have stellar character and companies that excel. But when someone or something looks too good to be true, he, she, or it *is*. The world is imperfect. Period. No one and no thing is without flaw, and if they appear that way, hit pause.

7- **Take their eyes off the big picture.** We function better emotionally and perform better in our lives when we can see the big picture. For successful people, no one event is ever the whole story. Winners remember that – each and every day.

8- **Neglect to do due diligence.** No matter how good something looks on the outside, it is only by taking a deeper, diligent, and honest look that we find out what we truly need to know: the reality we owe ourselves.

9- **Fail to ask why they are where they find themselves.** One of the biggest differences between successful people and others is that in love and in life, in relationships and in business, successful people always ask themselves, what part am I playing in this situation? Said another way, they do not see themselves only as victims, even when they are.

10- **Forget their inner life determines their outer success.** The good life sometimes has little to do with outside circumstances. We are happy and fulfilled most by who we are on the inside.

We all make mistakes. That's inevitable.

However, some mistakes have more impactful consequences that might allow us to get caught in a trap. It is what we do with the wisdom gleaned from being in the trap that creates the distinguishing mark between those who get out of the trap and "never go back" that makes the difference in our lives and legacies.

One common attribute, in addition to learning the lesson and never going back to the trap again, is the feeling of immense and almost overwhelming gratitude of ALL the women who shared their stories in this book. Grateful for escaping the trap, grateful for the lives they've reclaimed, grateful for the new outlook of understanding healthy, wholesome relationships.

In addition, most look younger than they've looked in years and feel better than they've ever felt. And there's a reason for that. According to Vivian Goldschmidt, MA, in her website www.saveourbones.com, there is scientific and medically-based research to support this. People who practice gratitude in plenty are healthier in five key ways:

1- Greater Happiness and Well-Being, Less Anxiety and Depression

When we cultivate a sense of gratitude, we can look forward to a happier, calmer outlook, according to a review published in *Clinical Psychology Review*. According to the research, gratitude is strongly linked to a sense of positive well-being, and "Well-being can be defined through (a)psychopathology (b)general emotional functioning

(c) existential functioning or (d) humanistic conceptions... Gratitude is robustly associated with each of these conceptions of well-being."

2- Leads to Lifestyle Habits Resulting In Better Health

It is interesting to note that grateful people tend to engage in healthful eating, regular exercise and other healthy habits. According to a 2013 study, "...Grateful individuals experience better physical health, in part, because of their greater psychological health, propensity for healthy activities, and willingness to seek help for health concerns."

These things feed on each other. Gratitude inspires healthy behavior, and healthy behaviors inspire more gratitude.

3- Builds a Strong Immune System

White blood cell counts are actually higher in those with a positive outlook, according to a study published in Psychological Science. Researchers evaluated law students as to positivity and optimism, and discovered that immunity was in fact influenced by outlook.

Those with an optimistic view had increases in various immune cells, leading researchers to note in their discussion, "Optimistic expectancies are accompanied by changes in immunity, as well as the first evidence for a mechanism by which this effect occurs."

4- Improved Sleep

When we are grateful, it is more likely we will get a good night's sleep (which is bound to make us even more thankful!). This was clearly shown in a study of 401 male and female participants, aged 18 to 68, which explored "pre-sleep cognitions" and how they influence sleep quality and duration.

Researchers report results that are independent of personality traits, including neuroticism, which can negatively affect sleep. The scientists note, "Gratitude predicted greater subjective sleep quality and sleep duration, and less sleep latency and daytime dysfunction." This elucidates prior research that revealed a remarkable improvement in mood and relaxation when people took time in the evenings to "count their blessings."

5- Healthier Relationships

Grateful people are more enjoyable to be around, and research shows they do in fact have healthier, more satisfying relationships. The study published in the Clinical Psychology Review found that grateful people practice positive relationship traits, such as forgiveness and interpersonal connection. Additionally, grateful people derive more satisfaction from their relationships. (Reprinted with Permission and Adapted from Saveourbones.com).

As treasure is being found, here's what the women in the stories you have read throughout the journey of this book are doing with their lives today:

One is traveling the world with her life love exploring the latest scuba diving destinations. Another is thriving in running two successful businesses and is married to someone she describes as, "The man who treats me better than I've ever been treated and who loves me unconditionally." One is raising a family of eight children, and multiplying their love for God and each other. While yet another is dancing blissfully each day with the freedom she longed to embrace for many years, with an added bonus of embracing a life of everyday adventure with the kindest man she's ever known.

And the one other thing they now have in common? They are all pillowing their heads each night knowing they are safe and free from the insecurities, addictions and mental inconsistencies that doomed the relationships and traps they once endured.

Freedom is the ultimate treasure.

BREAKTHROUGH MOMENTS

- What remnants did you choose to leave behind?

- How has this helped or even accelerated your healing process?

- What are the greatest gifts or treasures you now can claim as a result of being in the attractive trap?

- In what ways have these gifts made you a better person?

- What can you do, starting today, to begin serving others as a way to give back for the treasure you have received?

BREAK AWAY THOUGHTS

- Each and every day express gratitude for your freedom. Breathe it in.

- Freedom initially may have a high price – because it's worth it. The payoff and treasure will come.

- *"Freeing yourself was one thing, claiming ownership of that freed self was another."* "Beloved" by Toni Morrison

RESOURCES

United States Department of Veteran Affairs,
http://www.ptsd.va.gov/public/PTSD-overview/women/women-trauma-and-ptsd.asp

http://www.success.com/article/10-things-successful-people-never-do-again

"Never Go Back: The 10 Things You Will Never Do Again" by Dr. Henry Cloud

www.saveourbones.com

Made in the USA
San Bernardino, CA
20 December 2018